Uncommon Cents

Stories About Saving, Investing, and Everything in Between

JILL GLEBA

Copyright © 2023 by Jill Gleba

All Rights Reserved.
No part of this book may be reproduced in any manner
without the author's written consent except
in the case of brief excerpts in critical reviews and articles.

Inquiries about this book should be addressed to the publisher:

Jill Gleba
Troy, Michigan

Email: UncommonSense@JillGleba.com
Website: JillGleba.com

Uncommon Sense:
Stories About Saving, Investing, and Everything in Between

Written by Jill Gleba
Cover design & illustrations by Courtney Wollet | CourtneyWollet.com
Book design & editing by Karen McDiarmid Design, LLC | KarenMcDiarmidDesign.com

Printed at Color House Graphics | Grand Rapids, Michigan, USA

ISBN: 979-8-218-08171-3

Library of Congress Control Number: 2022918939

1. Personal Finance   2. Self Help   3. Parenting   4. Psychology

A book for the "finance curious" who want to learn more about personal finances
but aren't sure where to begin. Ideas and stories designed to help readers
make thoughtful money decisions, set goals, and take action.

10 9 8 7 6 5 4 3 2 1

*To my husband Bruce,
who didn't believe I could sit still long enough
to write a book*

*"Rich people stay rich by living like they are broke.
Broke people stay broke by living like they are rich."*

—*Anonymous*

CONTENTS

Introduction	7
Chapter 1 *What Are You Doing With Your Money?*	9
Chapter 2 *Motivation*	27
Chapter 3 *Kids and Money: Setting Them on the Right Path Early*	49
Chapter 4 *It's Not Gambling*	65
Chapter 5 *Careers: Finding Your Place*	83
Chapter 6 *Solving the Mysteries of College Costs*	93
Chapter 7 *Thinking of Starting Your Own Business?*	103
Chapter 8 *Retirement: Plan It and Make It Happen*	113
Chapter 9 *Taking Care of Yourself and Others*	133
Afterword *What's Next?*	147
About the Author & Illustrator	152

"Money is a resource to help you create more wealth and achieve the freedom to live the life you choose."

—*Jill Gleba*

INTRODUCTION

Think about money, just for a second.

Now ask yourself, "How did I like having that thought? Was it exciting? Stressful? Was I anxious? Or did I think about opportunities and possibilities?"

Maybe you thought, "I don't understand much about money, so I don't know what to think!"

Many people think the world of money and investment doesn't belong to them. But everyone can save. Everyone can invest. And everyone can do well with money.

Unfortunately, not everyone does, and there are a lot of reasons for this. One of the biggest reasons is the feeling that they don't belong in the saving-and-investing world. This feeling of insecurity leads many not to invest at all. They think investing is only for rich people. They don't know anyone who reads the *Wall Street Journal,* figuring it's only for CEOs and big-time stockbrokers. They've seen TV shows and movies in which everyone who has a stock portfolio also has a mansion, a butler, and a limousine. From this, they draw the tragic conclusion that the world of investing must be closed to them.

If this describes your thinking, then I'm writing this book for you! I want to turn around the notions you've accepted for much, if not all, of your life.

I want to challenge the idea that you don't make enough to save and invest. I want to push back on your belief that money management is a specialized skill that you can't possess. Let's upend any thoughts of money as a problem, and instead understand that money is a resource to help you create more wealth and achieve the freedom to live the life you choose.

Our financial health goes hand in hand with physical, mental, and social well-being. Think of these as the four pillars of health—physical, mental, social, and financial. In a workshop I once attended, we were asked to rate each of these four pillars on a scale of 1 to 10; 40 points was a perfect score. If your finances are suffering, your other pillars suffer as well. As I built my business, I noticed that when things were going well, we were very busy and my other pillars suffered. It is quite an achievement to keep all four pillars healthy and balanced. My intention is to give you the tools to create a great financial life, and hope that the other pillars will become stronger, too.

CHAPTER 1

What Are You Doing With Your Money?

"What are you doing with your money?"

What kind of question is that? You're putting it in the bank! You're paying bills! You're buying stuff!

What else would you do with it?

The answer might blow your mind. It did mine.

The answer opened my eyes and set me on a career path helping others understand that anyone—*anyone*—can successfully invest, regardless of circumstances or income.

More on that mind-blowing answer soon, but first, think about how you feel when opening your bills, looking at your savings, or otherwise considering how to plan for the future in what seems like such a challenging present. Do you feel fear and loathing? Do you have the common but misguided thought that you, like most people, simply can't afford to save or invest? Do you feel like all you can do is pay your bills and eat?

In the real-life situations I've seen, this is almost never true. Even those living on the most modest income can save something if they have a good plan and the discipline to stick to it.

When I got my first job out of college, I made $12,000 a year. With inflation, that's equivalent to earning around $36,000 a year today. The margin between my costs and income was small. But I was determined. Saving $85 a month, I was able to accumulate $1,000 over the course of a year (which was worth a lot more in the 80s).

That didn't leave a lot of extra money for food—let alone entertainment and impulse buys. But I made a choice. I knew there would be time later in my life when I could afford these extras, but my priority now was to position myself for the future. I could have applied for credit cards and bought just about anything I wanted. Had I done that, I'd have spent years—perhaps decades—dealing with credit card balances in addition to my normal, everyday expenses.

Instead, I chose to put myself on sound financial footing early in life, and I had the discipline to do it.

My point in sharing this story is not to say that I did something extraordinary. I didn't. It was something anyone can do. The difference was that I understood that I could do it. I saw myself as someone who could master money.

Random encounter rocks my world.

I was proud of myself for saving $1,000 over the course of the year with my modest income. Then, a chance encounter with a neighbor started the wheels turning.

"What are you doing with your money?" he asked.

"I'm putting it in the bank," I answered. "What else would you do with your money?"

He told me about this thing called a mutual fund. He explained that ordinary people could invest their money into funds that would then be used to purchase stock in companies—like "real" investors.

It seemed risky—a lot riskier than the bank. But my neighbor explained that this was a way to put my money to work for me. Still nervous, I was intrigued.

I did some research and thought, "Why not try?"

I identified a medical technology fund that looked interesting. Medical technology seemed like the sort of thing that would generate high demand. If I was going to try it, this would be my fund. I was off and running, like a real investor! I watched its performance in the *Wall Street Journal*.

But then, wait! Almost immediately after I bought it, the value went down!

"Dang it! I knew this was too risky!" I thought.

I marched right over to that neighbor's house. "Those mutual funds you told me about? I bought one," I said. "And it went down!"

He smiled.

I was confused. Why on earth was he smiling? I lost money! My hard-earned savings was gone!

"Excellent," he replied.

"Excellent? No, *not* excellent. I *lost* money!" And yet, there he stood—*smiling*.

"Buy more of it right away," he told me.

"Why would I do that?" I asked. "I just lost a bunch of money from the first round I bought."

"No, you didn't," he explained. "You're thinking about it all wrong."

He explained that unless I was planning to sell my shares right away, the fund's value going down didn't mean I had lost money. All it meant was that the price of the fund had gone down at that moment. Mutual funds always have ups and downs. The idea is to buy when the price of the fund is low so you can sell it when the price is high.

"If the price of the fund has gone down, it's an opportunity to buy more shares," he said.

I was apprehensive but his explanation made sense. I took his advice and bought more shares. Then, I waited.

"Patience is crucial for investing," he told me. "The trend is almost always up, but sometimes it takes a while to ascend."

I kept an eye on the fund and tried not to obsess over the ups and downs. Like he'd suggested, I focused on the trend. There were some down days (and even some down weeks), but the trend was consistently more up than down.

As time went by, I realized that the value of my investment in the fund had more than recovered from those initial losses. I also realized I'd benefited by buying those additional shares when my neighbor encouraged me to do so. I'd made even more on that investment because I paid less per share for it initially.

Letting fear get in the way of this opportunity would have cost me more than the money I made. It would have cost me an entire understanding of money and how I could make my money work for me.

It also ignited my career, helping other people do well with money. That experience set me on a lifelong learning journey.

Now I hope to show you how you can take the first steps on a journey of your own.

Now is the best time to start.

When we look at the money-making segment of our lives, the best-case scenario is that we'll earn enough so that someday, we won't have to work anymore. You might still want to—there are people who love working and hope they never have to stop. But there's a difference between working at the age of 70 because you love it and working at the age of 70 because you can't afford to quit.

You don't want to be in the latter situation. In fact, you'll ideally have the choice to stop working much earlier than age 70. It's very plausible. But you need a plan, and you need to work your plan with discipline and focus. Even before this, you must believe that you belong in the saving-and-investing world.

There are two ways to make money. You can work for it or invest it. These two potential sources of income are available to anyone. It's simply a matter of allocating some of your earnings, no matter how modest it may seem now, to fund investments. The best time to get started is now.

The sooner you start, the more money you can build, and the quicker you'll get used to the ups and downs of the market. These patterns are scary at first, but you'll soon become accustomed to them. In fact, you'll learn that those down moments are the best times to invest.

Think about the things you've learned that once seemed impossible. Do you remember when you learned to read? It's a complex system to master! The English language is confusing, with random rules and patterns. Yet, you learned it.

You learned other things, too. You learned to drive. Maybe you learned to cook or fix cars or build things. You might have learned to play a musical instrument. The truth is that learning good financial management isn't that much harder than learning any of these other skills.

Maybe those other skills don't seem quite as scary as money to you. Money can seem mysterious and foreboding. In your mind, playing a wrong note won't send you into bankruptcy, but making a mistake with your finances equals certain financial doom. If you burn dinner, you can order a pizza, but a bad investment will surely ruin you. These are misconceptions that prevent many people from mastering their finances and futures. Change your thinking and believe that you can do this—because you can!

Recognize your value.

The first way to make money is to work for it. But far too many people land a job earning an hourly wage and view their relationship with their employer as one in which they have no power. They're grateful to have the job and they should be—but they don't understand that the employer should also be grateful to have *them*.

So, let's talk about your value in the workplace. Perhaps you have more value than you think. I'm talking about quantifiable, inherent value. It's something that goes way beyond how many hours you work or how hard you work. It has to do with what you produce, and the value of it.

When your employer pays you $15 per hour (just to use an arbitrary figure), what do you think the employer is paying for? Do you think it's just for those 60-minute increments of your time? That's not it. The employer is paying for the *results* of the work you do, which are used by the company to help it make more money.

Consider an assistant to a real-estate broker. Let's say the assistant works six hours a day and prepares the information necessary for the broker to pursue deals on 25 listings. The broker would never have had time to do all this alone. But with the assistant's effort, the broker is able to aggressively pursue these sales and close deals on 10 of the listings in a single month. As a result, the broker earns commissions of $50,000.

Without the help of the assistant, the broker would only have been able to close on four of the listings and would only have earned commissions of $20,000. The assistant's help made it possible for the broker to earn an additional $30,000. And what was the assistant paid during that month? Only $1,800!

If the value of the assistant's work is understood, the assistant can do one of several things. The most obvious is to demand a raise. The broker would be foolish to say no because the broker doesn't want to lose $30,000 a month in commissions. Another option would be to look for a new position, with a broker who isn't making that additional $30,000 but would surely like to!

Understanding the value you bring to your employer puts you in a position to be better compensated because you'll know that the employer has as much need for you as you have for the employer.

What if you are working in a position that doesn't produce such apparent value? In that case, look for ways to provide value so you are positioned to earn more.

Let's say you answer the phones all day and transfer calls to people who solve customer problems. There's value to this, of course, but let's say you realize that you can solve many of the customers' problems yourself. This would save time and free up the other employees to be productive in other areas. You'd provide the company with more value and should be able to ask for better compensation. Because of your value, they'd be reluctant to see you go and would be more willing to consider compensating you for your work.

Most people don't think in terms of increasing their value. Most people show up, do their best, and hope the company will be generous enough to pay them a little more at some point.

With that thought process, most people are missing out. Companies benefit when they have useful and productive employees because it makes their company better. With some strategic thinking and serious effort, you can make yourself more essential and help the company reach its goals. This gives you *bargaining power*.

Earning more money isn't a matter of asking nicely, or of telling the boss how badly you need it, or of comparing what you make to what someone else makes. It's a matter of making certain the company *needs your value* and understanding what they lose without you. Once you understand your value and realize the power of what you do in the employment relationship, you can bargain for a decent return on the value you bring.

I realize this can be scary. What if they say no? What if you're seen as someone who rocks the boat? What if you lose your job?

These are scary thoughts, and I don't want to see anyone make demands without first being sure of the value they're bringing to the table.

I had an employee who once worked for my company. He was just a few years out of college when we hired him. He'd only been on the job for three months when he came to me and said, "I should be making $100,000 a year by now."

Oh?

Where was he getting this idea? As far as I could tell, he simply figured that people who work at financial planning firms and have high-level responsibilities are supposed to make that kind of money. He had no concept of the relationship between the value he was producing and the value he expected back.

"Okay," I replied. "What are you doing to create that?"

He didn't understand what I meant by the question. We walked through the various accounts he was responsible for and looked at how they were performing. I showed him that he was only producing about $20,000 a year in earnings for the company. He had never looked at it that way. He wanted to make $100,000, but he had no sense of the value he needed to produce to be worth that amount.

If you're certain of your value, however, then you have bargaining power. And remember, what you do for one employer, you can also do for another. The secret more people should know is that companies can always find people, but they struggle to find *good* people who really produce value.

Look for a pivot point.

As your career progresses, keep looking for ways you can pivot to your happy place. You spend a lot of time at work, so make the best of it. Look at your manager, other departments, and careers in other industries that may compliment your skills. Look around your company and ask yourself, "Is there an area of the company—perhaps marketing, finance, sales, or manufacturing—where I think I could do well and give the company solid value? Is this an area where I see myself growing and advancing?" It may be a good idea to talk to a career counselor or resume expert to help you explore ideas. Consider approaching someone who works in an area that interests you. Ask how they got to where they are and how you could do the same.

Is this prompting you to reconsider what you're doing and what you're getting paid for it? I certainly hope so. You might think about a different field entirely, something that would produce more value and be better rewarded. Search out top executives at the companies where you'd like to work on sites like LinkedIn. Then, contact them. Ask if you can visit their offices or meet for coffee. Explain that you're interested in their field and that you'd like to know what they can tell you about how to break into it.

Not all of them will meet with you, but you'll be surprised at how many are willing. Many of those executives entered their fields in a similar way and are happy to do for others what someone once did for them.

You have value to offer. You are worth your employer's time. Realizing this will build your confidence and propel you along the road to a healthy financial future.

It is easier to explore options while you have a job and can pay your bills. There's nothing to lose by investing time and energy exploring possibilities. You may discover you like where you are. You may choose to move on. Keep in mind that a move doesn't necessarily mean you'll receive a raise in pay right away, but it can lead to a more emotionally and financially rewarding career.

I spoke with a young person who worked as a software engineer in security. His hours were crazy, the money was great. Working 90 hours a week is not ideal, even if you're making great money. He found a way to improve his life. He changed careers to one that paid less but offered better hours. Within 4 to 5 years he caught up with his original salary. You might think of this as a step backward, but he didn't. He is much happier without the horrible hours and stress that was damaging his health. Keep striving for the ideal situation for you.

Ignore the myths!

Getting your career path on track and using your value to its full potential is one way you can start to master your finances. But the salary you earn is only one way to make money. The second is through smart, long-term investments. No matter how modest your income, you can still make your money work for you.

It might seem overwhelming at first. The media and popular culture have perpetuated a lot of myths about saving and investing. If you believe them all, you may decide to put your money under your mattress and be done with it.

Let's take a minute, right now, to knock down those myths.

Myth #1: The stock market is gambling.

One of the biggest myths in popular culture is the idea of "playing the stock market"— as if it's akin to roulette at your local casino. You might have the idea that it's all a gigantic gamble that could leave you penniless and begging for change on a highway exit ramp. The stock market isn't something you "play." Investing isn't a game. It's simply a series of decisions about where your money has the best potential to earn more value.

Myth #2: It's a con.

You might also have heard things that gave you the impression that the stock market is an attempt by con artists to make easy money without working. This phenomenon is made worse by actual con artists who claim to have unlocked "secrets" allowing you to make a killing overnight by following their formula. "No one knows this! Use my system and you'll make 10 times your money in less than a week! They're the secrets Wall Street doesn't want you to know!"

If you listen to enough of this nonsense, you could definitely start thinking the stock market really is a big game and that investing is only for those who like to gamble with their lives.

Investing is simply putting your money to work in companies and ventures that are trying to earn profit and create wealth. There's nothing mysterious about it.

Myth #3: It's a short-term venture.

Yet another myth is that it's all about short-term gains or short-term losses. There are those who think that, if you buy a stock in April and the stock is down in October, you "lost your shirt" or "took a bath" or whatever idiom you may have heard.

It can work that way. But that's not how smart investors think about it.

As a smart investor, you are in it for the long haul. You know that the trend is always upward but recognize that there will be downturns along the way. So just as that old neighbor of mine urged me long ago, when the price is down, good. Buy more. That's when you're getting the best value. The most important thing you can do is to stay with it and not panic over a short-term blip.

If you still have trouble understanding the wisdom of taking a long-term approach, consider this: What if there was a stock market for houses and every day your house at 3 Chestnut Lane was listed in the newspaper. Yesterday, it was listed at $401,000, and today it's $399,500?

Would you sell the house because it went down $1,500 in value? Of course not. Apply the same discipline to your investing.

I have some charts that illustrate the value of having a long-term perspective when you invest. The one below is an example of what would have happened to an initial investment of $10,000 during specific time periods. Notice that gains were realized in all but the years 2000-2009, the only negative decade since the S&P started. The point is, over the long term, the market will earn money most of the time.

Investment Period	End Value	Avg. Annual Return
January 1970–March 2022	$2,417,291	11.09%
January 1970–December 1979	$19,106	6.74%
January 1980–December 1989	$50,384	17.54%
January 1990–December 1999	$53,232	18.20%
January 2000–December 2009	$ 9,090	(.95%)
January 2010–December 2019	$35,666	13.56%

This is for illustration purposes only and does not conclude that there is any guarantee when you invest in the stock market.

Myth #4: Only the rich hire financial advisors.

You don't have to do it alone. There are reputable financial planners who can help you. That's exactly what they're for. They'll ask you about your goals. They'll learn how much risk you're comfortable with: Are you more cautious or do you want a more aggressive plan with more risk but with the possibility of a higher return? Are you bothered by market peaks and valleys? Based on these and a number of other criteria, they'll help you develop and implement a strategy to invest your money.

Do you think that help is only available to wealthy people? Not at all! Indeed, *most* people hire financial planners. There's tremendous value in having an ally who's done it before and knows how to think, strategize, and execute financial plans with your best interest in mind. One of the smartest things you can do is to hire someone to help who is more qualified than you are. If you can gain insight from someone who has experience, take full advantage! For instance, you might think that since I'm a financial planner, I do my own tax returns. Nope. I could, but I have a CPA who knows more than I do about taxes. I get better value by paying him to do it than by taking the time to do it myself. (Oh, and my CPA has help, too—all the smartest people do!)

Myth #5: I'm not rich enough to invest.

What about the myth that there's no point in investing unless you already have large amounts of money? This one's definitely not true either. You can absolutely start investing with small amounts of money. My kids started investing before they were teenagers. They didn't have a lot. But they invested what little they had, and they learned how it works.

So, why do people wait?

Those who choose not to invest are missing an opportunity to see their assets grow. I asked some of my clients why they didn't start earlier.

Some were nervous after hearing about unscrupulous financial advisors who were ripping people off. The more you hear about this sort of thing, the more reluctant you might become to trust anyone.

I would never tell you to trust just anyone flat-out, but you can get a sense of people by asking good questions, checking their references, and learning about their professional reputations and track records.

One of my clients had a bad experience buying a "guaranteed product" at a seminar. This married woman bought a "single life" annuity, which left her with no income after her husband passed. A reputable financial advisor would have learned about her situation and picked a product that actually met her needs instead of pushing something on her to make a sale.

Another client went to a seminar and bought a "specialty trust," thinking it would provide him with money if he needed to enter a nursing home later in life. The problem was that he still had kids in college, and it was way too early for him to tie up his money. The trust prevented the couple from selling their home and moving to northern Michigan—something they'd always planned to do.

Once again, the person who sold this man the product had no real understanding of his life situation. He just wanted to make a sale. This kind of thing makes people leery of investment advisors—and of investing at all.

Some clients said they hadn't invested earlier because they lacked the knowledge. But, of course, we all lack knowledge until we obtain it through education or experience. People who don't invest for lack of learning are missing the head start enjoyed by people who made a point of obtaining the education.

Others didn't invest because they lacked confidence in the outcomes. But, when you see that there are an awful lot of people doing well with investments, you can see that there are reasons to be confident. You just need to discover what they are.

When we talk about confidence in investing, it helps to understand a few things about the brain and your genetic makeup. Did you know that up to 40 percent of your confidence comes from your DNA? Three brain chemicals—oxytocin, serotonin, and dopamine—control our dispositions. We don't all have the same allocations, so some of us are literally born with more confidence than others. It can be developed, however, and the best way to do that it is to learn how something works.

A lot of people lack confidence when trying something new. Maybe it's a sport or even a job interview. If this describes you, try it anyway! Sometimes things don't work out, but sometimes you discover you had more to offer than you ever imagined. Your decision to give it a shot could be life-changing. Imagine stepping back to consider that you almost didn't apply for that job or didn't try out for that team.

Some clients did get started in investing early, learning the basics in high school or college. One client learned to invest when her high school teacher held a stock contest. The teacher asked each student to pick a stock and follow its progress throughout the semester. This showed her the potential of investing, and before long, she got started with the real thing. Several clients of mine learned the basics of investing from a high school teacher or a college professor. It's very satisfying to think that one person opened the door to the rewards of investing for so many.

There should be more classes in schools that teach financial planning, but until there are, be thankful for people in your life from whom you can learn—a teacher, an uncle, a boss, or a wise neighbor. If you weren't lucky enough to have those mentors in your life, all is not lost. There are a lot of places where you can learn the basics. For example, the Small Business Administration has classes for business owners, and many of them teach about investing.

Of course, you need to be careful who you listen to along the way. I had a client some years back—during the dot-com boom—who needed to rebalance her portfolio. During the process of working through this with her, she changed course and listened a colleague who gave her some advice while chatting at the water cooler. He told her tech stocks were hot and said she should put all her money in technology. Against my advice, she did. One month later, she called me in tears. She had lost 70 percent of her 401(k) portfolio. When I asked what that work colleague had to say about what happened, she said his reply was, "Oops."

Oops is right.

Knowledge trumps fear.

Want to overcome your fear of investing? Start by doing some reading. Read up on money, saving, financial planning, and financial markets. I realize it may sound dry and boring, but maybe that's because you've never taken the opportunity to learn about it. I know a guy who declared for years that he hated beets, but when pressed, he had to admit he couldn't remember ever trying one. (He said they turned out better than he expected, although I'm not sure he'll ever really be a fan.)

Obviously, you've got a start already—you're reading this book, after all! When you're done with it, let me recommend another one. It's called *The Energy of Money: A Spiritual Guide to Financial and Personal Fulfillment*, by Maria Nemeth. It's as much about psychology as it is about money—the psychology of how people look at money and how that influences where they spend it.

Published in 1998, the principles it presents are timeless. It looks at the changing patterns and beliefs that lead you to self-defeating ideas and behavior where money is concerned. It will challenge many of your deep-seated assumptions about life.

I read Nemeth's book when I was well into my career as a financial planner. It helped me recognize the need to encourage young people to start saving early and to focus on simple things like saving earnings from their first part-time job or maintaining a job when they are in college. One of the best lessons you can teach your loved ones is to start investing at a young age.

There are plenty of other things you can read—some better than others. Most important is understanding that money is something you can learn about and master, rather than something that masters and scares you.

How do you find help?

If you don't know what you are doing, it may be best to hire a professional. How do you find a reputable financial planner—one you can trust and with whom you are comfortable? Get referrals. Call a neighbor, friend, or family member and ask them if they work with someone. Then find out, on a scale of 1–10 (with 10 being the best), if they like working with them. If they do, interview them. Interview several. Be cautious and make sure they ask you a lot of questions about your current situation and your goals. Be certain they have your best interest in mind and that they're not just trying to sell you something. Unfortunately, it happens. I've already shared a few stories from my clients. Here's another example of a situation where an "expert" lead a client down the wrong path.

This particular woman was determined to find a way for her money to make more than just the interest she was earning on her savings account. She bought a fund from her bank. She knew nothing about investing and the bank seemed the logical place to start. She was completely inexperienced. She knew nothing about the number of funds and choices out there. She assumed the bank would find the best option for her. They suggested a fund that, over many years, never earned more than she had by keeping it in her savings account. It wasn't the right fund but her conclusion was that investing wasn't worth the time. She didn't discover that they'd misguided her until years later after speaking with me.

- They did not ask her why she was investing or what the money was for.
- She was not presented with options, just one fund.
- She came to us because it was not making money after several years.
- She wanted a fund for growth, not something similar to a bank account.

Another couple inherited some money and called us because they wanted to invest it. They'd already seen another advisor and, before acting, wanted a second opinion. The first advisor had suggested an income fund—with no questions asked.

We did some digging. We asked a lot of questions. We learned that they were looking for growth with their money. This immediately told us that the product that had been recommended by the first advisor was not a good fit for them. On top of that, they had a lot of expensive debt and no money set aside for emergencies. We didn't invest their money. Instead, our advice to them was to use half of the inheritance to pay off their debt and to put the other half in the bank to cover emergencies. This was the right decision for this couple.

When you've found your advisor, you can take comfort in the fact that they are there to help and are your ally in your pursuit to build wealth for your future.

Put knowledge and a plan to work.

Here's one of my favorite examples of how important it is to have a plan, and to stick to it. I knew a couple who lived in a middle-class neighborhood. He worked as a mechanic, and she was a nurse. Each of them earned about $50,000 a year. They decided to live solely on the income from one of their salaries and save the income from the other. This left them about $4,000 each month for living expenses.

They had three kids. They had a modest house. Occasionally they would draw from the second income to pay for vacations, but that exception was built into their plan, and they were very disciplined about sticking to it.

They put all three kids through college. Today, they're both retired and happy. How did they do it? By having a plan and sticking to it. As far as I'm concerned, they're rich, because they found a way to have the life they wanted and are living it.

Another couple came to me—still in their 20s—with serious debt on their hands. A lot of financial planners had declined to even meet with them because they didn't see much potential for this couple to become lucrative clients. Call me crazy, but I thought I could make a difference for them, and I wanted to help.

Once they described their situation, I saw a path out for them. I told them it wouldn't be easy. But, if they were willing to do it, they could emerge from their debt.

They each had a full-time job. I told them that, if they each added a part-time job earning them an additional $400 a month, they could put that extra income toward retiring the debt and be done with it in three years. Without question, this would be hard work. They would have to give up free time and a lot of leisure activities. The payoff, however, would be tremendous.

They did it. After they retired that debt, they stepped back and realized they were not only financially free, but they had also discovered skills they didn't realize they had.

Another client started out as the fry guy at McDonald's. You might think there's not much opportunity to prove your value in a job like this, but he thought otherwise. He showed up on time every day. He worked hard. He learned the McDonald's system. Eventually, he became a manager, making $65,000 a year.

He didn't stop there. Today, he owns three McDonald's franchises.

What set any of these people apart from the rest of the population? What they did required hard work and discipline, but they weren't executing some secret formula impossible for the average person to understand. It was simply a matter of looking at the numbers, applying the numbers to their situations, and then coming up with a plan they could stick with.

It starts with believing. And I'm telling you now that you can do it, too. I'm basing this on my personal experience working with many clients who never imagined they could achieve the money goals they had.

Are you motivated? Get started!

You don't need to be a financial genius. Understanding money—how it works, what to do with it, how to put it to work for you—is not so difficult.

As an investor, you can't control the market, but you can control your attitude toward the market. You can understand that the ups and downs are part of the process and recognize the opportunities inherent in each. Don't watch the news if the way they cover the markets makes you nervous. Learn the patterns and recognize that, in any given 10-year period, there will likely be seven up years and three down years.

Make up your mind not to fret about the three down years—that's how the market works. It's correcting itself when it gets overheated. The market lost money in only one 10-year period since 1926, so stick with it.

Are you motivated to get started? Then learn about money and pursue your goals with patience and perseverance. There are few things you can learn in life that will reward you more than this.

"Actively saving and investing can give you peace of mind about retirement."

—**Jill Gleba**

CHAPTER 2

Motivation

I once had a client who wanted a big, beautiful wedding. So, she came up with a plan to save money, a little at a time, to afford the day of her dreams. She was focused. She was disciplined. She knew how much she needed to save each month, and she did it. When the day of her wedding arrived, no one was disappointed. It was classy and memorable, and she paid for the whole thing from the money she worked so hard to save.

Once she was married, you might think that continuing to save with the same financial discipline would be a slam dunk. After all, if she could save like that for her wedding, she could just as well keep up the same good practices to get a start toward her retirement.

You might think that was something she'd do. But you'd be wrong.

She saved all the money for her wedding for one simple reason—she really wanted it.

It had been her dream for a long time, and when she found herself with the opportunity to make it happen, nothing was going to stop her.

When it came to planning for retirement, the motivation simply wasn't there. She was still in her 20s. Retirement was decades away. There were other things she and her husband wanted to do with their money and their lives.

The discipline that had been so sharp in preparation for her wedding quickly melted away. Soon, all that extra income she'd been packing away was spent on here-and-now desires.

Maybe she'd get back on track. I certainly hoped so. She'd lost some ground, but she still had time.

Let's think about what happened. The savings required to set up her retirement would have been the same as what she'd been putting away for her wedding. We knew she was capable; she'd proven it.

The problem for her, and for many others, was not the lack of ability—it was the lack of motivation. Saving and investing requires knowledge, but just about anyone can learn it. It requires discipline, but just about anyone can do it. It also requires motivation, but not everyone can find it.

The reward for this couple from saving and investing successfully would be a happy retirement in which they could recreate their income while no longer working. They simply didn't want this future badly enough to stay motivated.

This is not to say they'd object to this future—few would. But in the here and now, it simply was not their priority. When you think of it in terms of human psychology, it's not that hard to understand. The woman who saved for her wedding could expect to receive the gratification for her efforts quickly. And when she did, it was spectacular.

When saving in your 20s for a payoff that won't come until you're in your 60s, you'll have to accept that there won't be short-term gratification. You'll spend many years looking ahead to that reward. It's easy to convince yourself that there's no hurry. And it's easy to want to spend the money you have today on things you can enjoy today.

But there is a reward today when you plan for tomorrow. Most people worry to some degree about how they'll pay for retirement, even those who aren't saving and aren't working toward a plan. Whether they're procrastinating or they just don't think they have the spare money to put away, it's still in the back of their minds. They don't have a plan, and it troubles them.

Actively saving and investing can give you peace of mind about retirement. There's real value in that. Unfortunately, it doesn't always inspire the motivation needed to make planning for the future a priority.

What's stopping you?

Clients often look to me for help breaking through the psychological barriers that prevent them from forming a financial plan.

"My parents died at a young age, and they never had any money," someone might say. "Why bother?"

In this case, the person hasn't seen saving and investing work for anyone close, making it hard to envision the rewards that make it all worthwhile.

Then, there's immediate gratification. This often keeps people disconnected from the kind of good fiscal discipline that would help achieve larger goals, such as retirement.

I had a client, some years ago, who wanted to buy a car—a car he chose because he associated it with being rich and successful. He had a set number in mind for the purchase price he expected to pay. However, he hadn't considered what his monthly payments would be, or how they would fold into a monthly budget.

As we talked, I presented the numbers to him. He looked at me like I was an alien. We had to go over it three times before he was finally able to wrap his head around this kind of thinking.

It's not uncommon for people to be motivated to make purchases for reasons like this. They want to buy things they think will make them look successful before they really are successful. This fellow started with a motivation that had little or nothing to do with long-term financial strength. Driving that car may have made him feel like he'd made it, but it was an illusion. The impact of his financial decision would catch up with him.

It's easy to fall into this trap. You might qualify for financing to get a nice car. You can use your credit card to squeeze in the purchase of some very fancy clothes while still staying under your limit. Maybe you qualify for the purchase of a very nice home with no money down. You can even get an 18-month, interest-free loan for the furniture to fill that nice home.

There are so many incentives out there that encourage bad financial decisions. And there are unscrupulous people and companies who seduce consumers to take advantage of these incentives.

The mortgage officer gets a bigger commission when you qualify for a house you can't really afford. Human decency might motivate that person to caution you against overextending yourself, but economic incentives will not.

How do you protect yourself from falling prey to these temptations? It comes down to understanding what it really means to be wealthy.

What is wealth?

Is wealth a lifestyle? Is it something other people notice? Is it the nicest house on the block or the newest car? Is it the parties you throw or the places where you go out to eat? Maybe it's the vacations you take and the exotic photos you post on social media?

If you believe wealth means having other people recognize you as wealthy, you can see why these might be the measures you'd embrace. But if wealth means having a strong underpinning of resources that you manage well and deploy responsibly, that's another matter entirely.

Not long ago, a couple with whom my husband and I are friends came for a visit. They arrived with great fanfare, quite excited because they had just bought a new car. We were excited for them. We walked outside, checked out the car, admired all the bells and whistles, and then went inside to pop a bottle of champagne for the occasion.

I thought we'd been quite celebratory, but before long, the wife of the couple surprised me by saying, "You're hard to impress."

I told her I wasn't sure what she meant. She explained that, while we seemed happy enough about their new car, we didn't seem terribly impressed. Maybe that's because we weren't—although I certainly thought we did a good job of pretending we were.

I don't mean it wasn't a nice car. It was very nice. But things like cars don't impress us.

If you have a nice car that you like, and it performs well for you, I am very happy for you. But if you're buying a car with hopes of impressing others, I'm probably not going to give you what you want. That's simply because I've seen people do many things with money for the wrong reasons. Trying to impress people is the wrong motivation.

As a financial advisor, I want my clients to be wealthy in the classic sense. I want them to have income that exceeds their expenses. I want them to have plenty of money saved—and not just money saved, but money working for them. I want them to be able to do the things they'd like to do without sweating it, but I don't want them to view the things they buy or the experiences they have as the measurements of their lives.

Buying more and better things will not satisfy you. If you can change your thinking from here-and-now gratification to long-term financial strength, you'll eventually find out that delayed gratification is sweeter.

How do you think about money?

How you think about money has a lot to do with your reaction when encouraged to save money. Psychologists have identified three mindsets that lead to resistance. It helps to identify your own patterns of thinking and recognize how they might be inhibiting your motivation to save and invest.

Not another obligation!

"I have to" people see investing as an unwelcome obligation. They are dragged into it kicking and screaming. They feel like they're being forced to save or invest. They're never really going to recognize the value of it until they understand that there's nothing they truly "have to" do.

Something new? No thanks!

Those who resist investing because it is unfamiliar might recall when they first learned to ride a bike. "How can that thing stay up on only two wheels?" they might have wondered. Yet, they learned to balance, and it soon became natural. Investing is the same way.

What if I fail?

The only real answer for those who fear failure is to accept that there are no guarantees. By becoming familiar with the track record of the markets, they will hopefully recognize that success is far more likely, as long as they stick with a plan and stay in it for the long haul.

It helps to understand that it's okay not to be a "perfect" investor. There will be ups and downs. There might even be mistakes. That's okay. Everyone makes them. Don't hold yourself to such a high standard that you remain an ever-anxious investor and prevent yourself from building a solid, long-term portfolio.

Then there's the opposite of the resistors.

On the other end of the spectrum is the gambler. Gamblers have no resistance to investing and are one of the more difficult clients. They are impulsive investors who "play the market" (as if it's a casino game) and embrace the thrills instead of embracing sound strategies. They will put everything into one investment, hoping for a big payoff. They pour money into a stock that just went down, expecting an immediate and substantial return.

Gamblers operate on hunches, not on research or expert advice. Even favorable markets are dangerous for them because gamblers are prone to extreme risks, and they don't cover those risks sufficiently.

Most of the gamblers I know can tell you stories of phenomenal trades they've made, but I don't know any who have come out ahead in the long run.

Find financial, physical, and mental well-being.

Money is a leading source of angst for Americans, with many being stressed about finances at least some of the time. Stress is a natural response to serious situations or danger, but if finances make you feel helpless and stress is ongoing, it can disrupt mental and physical health. Ongoing or severe financial stress can lead to sleeplessness, depression, headaches, unhealthy coping choices, and a weakened immune system.

Having tools to help you manage finances allows you to plan for your future.

It can relieve stress and improve overall health. You can give yourself a sense of financial security by:

- Having a long-term plan and sticking with it.
- Meeting financial obligations.
- Spending wisely.
- Steadily building savings for long- and short-term goals.
- Adhering to your values; buying things because they're important to you, not to impress others.
- Surrounding yourself with like-minded, positive people.

Doing these things will give you a sense of security and accomplishment. This feeling is personal. It's not to impress others. Focus on yourself, and when you have enough in the bank to cover that next emergency, instead of stress, you will enjoy the freedom of greater choices.

Understand your cash flow.

So, how can you stay ahead of the curve and learn to make more thoughtful money decisions? Let's talk about your cash flow, how you can assess where your money is going, and how that affects your long-term goals.

One of my clients struggled to save. After taking a hard look, she realized that she spent a lot of unnecessary money shopping for things she didn't really need. This was a problem because it wasn't only about the things she was buying. It was also about the experience and the friends she was spending time with while doing it.

She made a change by enlisting the help of her friends. They started spending time together while doing other things. They helped her—and probably themselves—create healthier financial habits.

Another client had a similar problem. Going out to the bar with friends was a big part of his lifestyle, and a lot of his income was funding this habit. He and his friends made a significant change. They started hanging out regularly in their homes. Everyone brought their own drinks and snacks and they socialized while playing video games. This simple lifestyle change saved him $200 a week.

Spending money mindlessly isn't uncommon. Workers may deposit their paycheck in the bank, pay their bills, and then spend the rest of it throughout the week. When it's gone, they wait for the next paycheck and do it all again. Need a car? They may see if they have money in the bank or just take out a loan. As a society, we're pretty stuck on making monthly payments instead of taking the time to understand the total cost of a purchase. It's much wiser to save for a car ahead of time. Then, when you need one, you can shop around armed with a substantial down payment and put a lot less stress on your cash flow.

Fill out your cash-flow chart.

Often, my clients are surprised when I walk them through a standard cash-flow discussion. I base it on a simple cash-flow chart (opposite). It's a great tool, and I love how working through it inspires ideas that flow from the heart and soul. Seeing goals in writing is a real motivator and the chart will allow you to easily see if everyday spending is making your extra money disappear and keeping you from reaching your goals.

Use it to analyze your monthly flows of income and spending. At a glance, you'll see what's going into your bank account and know if you have extra funds available. When filling it out, take time to think about what is important to you. Think about the things you want and need now (immediate); what needs you'll have in the next year (emergency fund); what you might need in 3-5 years (intermediate fund); and how much money is going into your retirement accounts. Often, retirement funds are deposited as a percentage of your paycheck directly into an employer retirement plan *before* you ever see them. If this is the case, there's not a spot for it on this chart, but write it down in the "Retirement" box to remind yourself that you are contributing to this segment of your life.

The top of the chart is where you'll record the income that flows into your account. On the left side of the chart, write down the expenses and bills that flow out of your account. The difference between these two numbers is your extra cash flow.

Now your income is divided into what's needed to cover expenses and the "extra"—what's left over after expenses. We'll talk more about how you'll use the

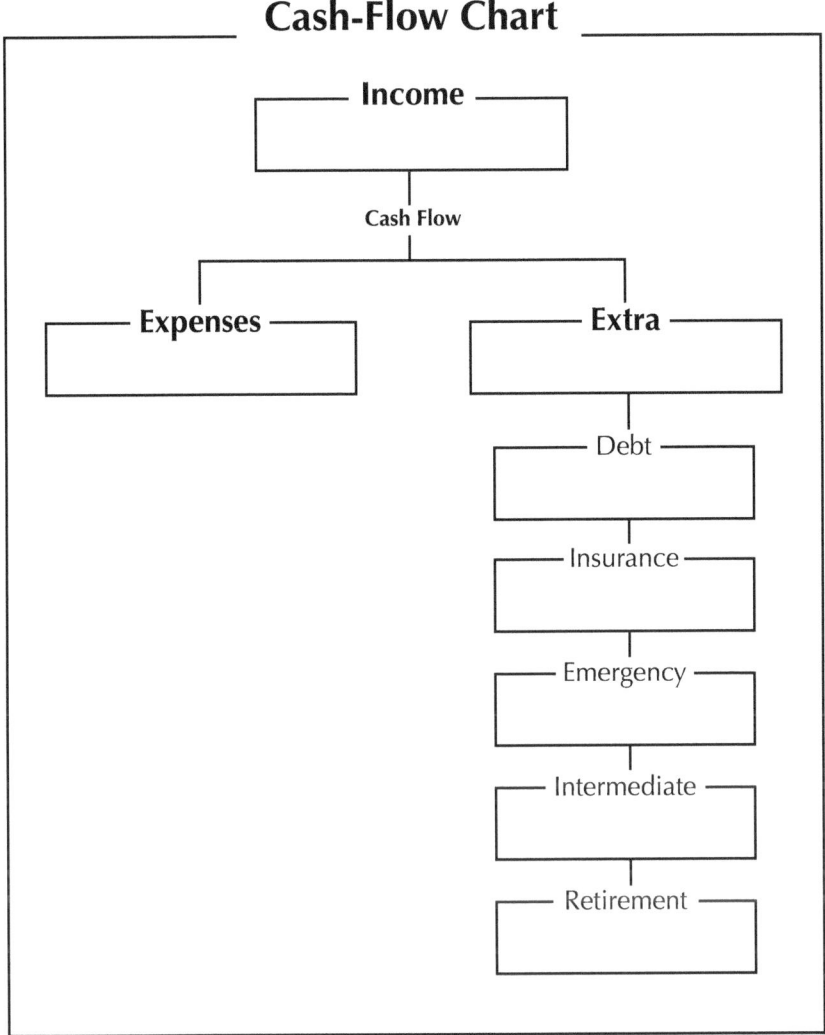

"extra" after you take some time to consider your goals. Start by writing down the things that are important to you. You might think of this chart as your decision tree. Motivation should come easily once you have a clear picture.

Maybe you're starting to see why this is my favorite part of financial planning! It's all about *you*! How often does that happen?

A very smart young man told me that his parents taught him to save, but what he was saving for, he never really knew. Why was he saving this money?

Lack of direction can be very confusing. It's motivating to have a clear idea of what you are saving for, and how long it may take you to get to that next step. It takes away stress by just "knowing" that you're making progress.

When investing the money you're saving, it's important to have an intention for it. There are appropriate investments for goals based on the time horizon, risk tolerance, and the taxes you'll incur based on the investments.

It is true that sometimes you are saving for intermediate-term goals (things you won't need for 3-5 years), and you might not know exactly what you are saving for, but that's okay. Believe me, something will come up and you'll be glad you have it!

Now let's take a closer look at how you'll use your "extra" funds, breaking them up into five categories: debt service, insurance, what's put away for emergencies, intermediate-term goals, and the longest-term need—retirement.

1. Debt—Get rid of it!

A couple came to me asking for advice. They earned $5,000 per month. I asked them how much they spent. Their answer? $5,000 a month! They weren't even thinking about saving.

Like many others, this couple was carrying debt. Their priority had to be paying it down. I told them to categorize their liabilities—showing the balances owed, the monthly payments, and the interest rate of each one—then pay them off, starting first with the most expensive debt or the lowest amount owed. Once an account was paid up, they could use the extra money to save or to pay off the next one. Their goal should be to have only their home as debt.

Credit card debt is very common, and I want all my clients to think about eliminating it. I sometimes make a not-so-serious suggestion.

"You owe $2,000 on a credit card? How about if I loan you $2,000, and at the end of the year you can pay me back $2,400?"

They usually look at me like I'm crazy—and that's exactly the reaction I want! When you run up credit card debt, that's the deal you're making with the credit card company. Getting rid of that debt is a priority, and income beyond expenses should first be used to pay off those balances.

It's not uncommon to see high levels of credit card debt—$20,000 or more. Yet, there's little motivation to pay it off. It's not all that painful to make the minimum payments, after all. This is shortsighted and is only putting off the day when a lot more money than was originally borrowed will be necessary to get rid of that balance.

Let's just say you had a credit card debt of $20,000 and figured out a budget that allowed you to put $500 each month toward the debt repayment. That would be $6,000 a year. It still might take you three or four years to pay off $20,000, but you'd be making progress.

Hopefully, you have no credit card debt, or only a small amount, to pay off—an amount that can be taken care of in a single year. In this case, you can fill out the chart and start thinking about other desires.

Often, people find that even if they have an extra $1,000 a month, it doesn't seem like enough to cover all their goals. That's normal. No matter what you have, it doesn't feel like enough.

Maybe you'd like to take some trips or do some other things that will take away from your "now" fund. Maybe, in the next year, you'll need to start paying for someone's college, need a new car, or want a new couch. Even by saving $300 a month for your "later" goals, it might take longer than you thought.

This is even more reason to be careful about things like a quick trip to Target or buying that fancy coffee. These little things might make the difference between saving a few hundred dollars every month or saving nothing.

Maybe you wait to buy the couch until you've put $500 a month into the "now" fund for a year, and then you have money for the couch with some extra for the next goal.

When you have a limited income, it becomes that much more important to spend your money on the things that really matter to you. Of course, having little or no debt makes it easier to make decisions about how to allocate your money.

2. Insurance

Insurance is used to protect your assets. There are many types for many different purposes. You might think it's boring and unnecessary. I get it. But inadequate insurance—health insurance, in particular—has caused serious financial hardships for many. Health issues can cost hundreds of thousands of dollars and create devastating financial scenarios from which some are unable to recover. In worse-case scenarios, uninsured persons have lost the ability to afford their homes and were forced to live in vehicles. It's scary and eye-opening—and a good reason to find an insurance expert and learn what's available and why you need it.

Here are some types of insurance you might consider:

- **Home and auto insurance** should be discussed with a property and casualty agent. Be sure you have adequate liability, and if you have young drivers at home, consider an umbrella insurance policy that would cover claims in excess of regular homeowners and auto policy coverage. Understand your policies and review your coverage annually.

- **Life insurance** protects your loved ones from losing your income when you pass. It allows them to pay off debt and complete goals, such as college funding, if you die prematurely. A financial planner can help you determine your needs.

- **Disability insurance** is often overlooked. If your income is supporting a family, this would protect your income should you become disabled. It's often offered in the workplace along with health insurance.

- **Long-term care insurance** is often purchased later in life to cover the cost of nursing-home care. The premium is typically much less if purchased when you are young, but that doesn't mean you should run out and buy it when you're in your 20s. After all, you won't likely need it until you are much older. If bought too early, you'd end up paying a lower price but for a much longer period of time. If you determine that this insurance is right for you, learn what's available. Some policies are paid with a monthly premium, and if it turns out that you never need it, you lose it. Hybrid policies allow you to pay a lump sum or a premium over 10 years. It's combined with an annuity or life insurance and, if long-term care isn't needed, the annuity or life insurance is paid to your family.

3. Planning for the unexpected

If you have little or no debt hanging over you, it's time to put together a plan for the unexpected. Ideally, aside from your house and car, your debts are paid off. At this point, a good rule of thumb is to tuck away three- or four-months' worth of income into the bank.

This stash of cash could change your life. Let's say your furnace goes out. This is a miserable situation to think about, but it's real life. If you have no emergency-money saved, you'll end up putting that furnace on a credit card or borrowing money from someone. Then, you're back to dealing with debt. On the other hand, with emergency-money saved, you can pay cash for the furnace. That's what it's there for!

4. Intermediate-term goals

What about the big things you'll know you want or need in the next few years? Maybe you'd like a new car in three or four years. Start redirecting some of your income to a car fund. Maybe you'd like to renovate your kitchen at some point. Start putting money away today. In a few years, that sparkling new kitchen is yours.

Your intermediate goals are more long-term, so it may be several years before you need this money. If you can handle the risk, invest this money in a conservative or balanced portfolio. You'll earn a bit more over the years, and if necessary, you can wait out a market downturn before buying the new car or committing to a home improvement project. Invest this money in a non-retirement account. You do not want your money to be tied up long-term since you'll be using it before retirement. You will pay taxes on the gains, but your money is available when you need it.

Are you starting to feel motivated? Do you recognize how the woman who wanted her elaborate wedding felt? Like her, you can envision the rewards of saving and get motivated by them!

5. Retirement—Investing in your future

Now let's talk about those retirement goals. You'll typically start with a workplace retirement plan like a 401(k) or 403(b), an IRA, or an annuity. Retirement products usually require you to wait until you are 59.5 years old to access your money, so understand that its purpose is for the future. Its not designed to use right away. Don't look at your retirement plan as a savings account. Just leave it alone. Let it grow so it can provide income in your retirement years.

Choose the right investments.

An advisor can help you choose appropriate investments. I realize this can be tricky. For someone with debt, you may be using half of your extra money to pay off what you owe and depositing the other half in the bank. Maybe it seems like you're not making progress, but soon you will see the debt go down and eventually disappear. Then, you can move on to your other goals. The point is, you're looking ahead, and you have a plan. Often, the biggest hurdle is expectations that are too high.

One client walked into my office and said he didn't see why he should keep putting money into his investments because they weren't growing. We pulled up his account. The investments had absolutely been growing. He looked surprised, yet he was still not satisfied. He was expecting something unrealistic, like 50 percent annual growth. Investments grow in value, but they take time. People need to understand the likely trends of the market, so they'll enter the investing world with realistic expectations.

Back in 2008, a prospective client walked into my office and said he wanted to move his account from another advisor because his portfolio had just lost money. I would have been happy to have him as a client, but it was 2008. Everyone's investments lost money that year. If he stuck it out—with the other advisor or with me—he would make his money back.

Here is the lesson. You need to be patient. After writing down your goals in each box, you may realize that you have a lot of goals! That's okay. Now your goals are separated into categories and timelines. This will help you decide how to invest this money, if at all. For instance, your emergency fund should be in the bank. If an emergency should arise, you do not want to deal with the ups and downs of the market. As a side note, some people use an open equity line in case of emergencies. Not a bad idea to have this available, however, you still need to have money in the bank!

Not everyone has a clear vision of what they want for their future, or how to achieve it.

A woman in her 60s came to me with $100,000 she'd recently inherited. The sudden windfall left her feeling very anxious. When she visited my office, she literally couldn't sit still. She paced. She wanted to shove the check in my hands and be done with it. "Here, just do something with it," she said.

I had just met her, however, and I couldn't just randomly invest her money. I didn't know her goals. In fact, at that time, *she* didn't know her goals!

"Let's take some time," I said.

I told her to go home for now. I suggested that she deposit the money into her bank, and to really think about what she wanted this money to do for her.

"Come back to see me after you've had time to think about it. It's crucial to understand your goals before investing."

When she came back, her thoughts were clear. She asked if we could develop a strategy so that her inheritance money would allow her to travel regularly. Home improvement projects didn't interest her, and the list of other things friends had suggested weren't high on her list either. She wanted to travel.

"Yes, we can make that happen," I told her. And we did.

She's in her 70s now, and she's taking vacations every year with the interest she earns from her investments. She sends pictures and tells me I made it happen, but I didn't. She made it happen by being disciplined and sticking to her plan. We've been working that strategy for more than 10 years.

Let's talk about a home purchase.

A young couple came to me, motivated to buy their first home. We talked about how much they could spend, and how much they should borrow. You don't want to drain your bank account when you buy a home since there are other things to purchase after you move. My general rule is to not borrow more than two times your annual income. Mortgage and real-estate professionals may want you to spend more, but I will caution you not to cave in.

For example, another couple came to me after they'd already purchased a home—their dream home. Unfortunately, they simply did not have the means to buy the house they bought. They were so wrapped up in the dream that they didn't care that they had no emergency fund, or that she was in danger of losing her job. When she did lose her job, their dream turned into one big mess. They sold the home at a loss and moved in with her parents until they could catch up on their finances. It was a huge disappointment for them, but they were smart enough to take my advice and get their finances in order so their next home purchasing experience would be a happy one.

Stick to your budget. When you buy a house, you will need your money for other things, too. If you don't know where your career is going, or if there's a possibility you may need to relocate, maybe you wait. Renting does not require paying taxes or the expense of upkeep. With a roommate, it can be a less expensive option while you figure things out.

In the beginning of his career, my son Robert moved to a different apartment seven years in a row. He spent time working overseas, so it was nice to have roommates who took care of the apartment. He had a place to come back to in between his travels.

When he grew weary of moving from apartment to apartment, he bought a condo. Then, he met his girlfriend and decided it was time to buy a home. She came with a dog, and dogs were not allowed in the condo. When he was single, the condo was a great choice for his lifestyle. A home has a different feel to it and it's important to think about your lifestyle when choosing a home.

Sometimes, market conditions will throw a wrench in your plans. It happened to me twice. I bought a home and the sale of the home I thought was sold didn't go through. Both times, I ended up with two homes for several months. My advice? Plan for the unexpected!

How to handle a sudden windfall.

Then there are those who make it big at the casino, win a lottery, or come into another big windfall. Getting a big payoff might seem like the ultimate solution: No more money worries! Yet, according to the National Endowment for Financial Education, about 70 percent end up bankrupt within a few years.

I'd like to say I find this surprising, but I don't. People who come into large amounts of money without having worked out a strategy aren't prepared for that kind of wealth. They don't appreciate how important it is to be responsible with it, and they don't understand just how limited their newfound assets really are.

Also, they have a skewed idea of what it means to be rich. It makes them feel better to have a lot of money, and they want to indulge that feeling by spending it on things that they think rich people do. They've never learned about good financial management, and too often, they don't have people in their lives who can help them with it. That's especially true if they haven't grown up around people who have mastered these good habits.

There's a psychology that makes people want to live somewhere nicer, bigger, and better than where their parents grew up. That's one of the reasons young couples jump at lavish homes after qualifying for massive mortgages with nothing down. It makes them feel like they've jumped classes.

Yet, it's rare for people to jump classes. I'm not saying it can't be done. One of the primary reasons I'm writing this book is to show that it can be done. But it is rare because of the struggle to leave the psychology of the class from which we came.

How you think about money.

Middle-income people are trained to think about money in a certain way. It's not the same way upper-income people think about money. Their habits and instincts are different. Unlearning these behaviors and embracing new ones is the key to elevating oneself financially, but it's a hard thing to do.

There are also differences between the way men and women think about money. In general, women tend to have a greater fear of ending up in the poor house. If a few things go wrong, they envision themselves being homeless bag ladies. There's a very palpable fear of running out of money—even for women who have a lot of it.

I am not exempt. To this day, when I go shopping with my husband, I might see a sweater I really like. It might be a little nicer and pricier than some of the other sweaters, but he can tell I want it. He'll implore me, "Just buy it!"

But that's not the way I was taught to think. My mother didn't take me on shopping sprees for clothes. We got clothes on our birthdays and on Christmas—not just because we felt like it. This ideal is ingrained in my mind.

"Do I really need this?" I ask myself.

You might think this is crazy, but I've seen excess spending get a lot of people in trouble. They buy homes they can't really afford. Their shopping trips get out of control. They have the latest clothes, but they also have sleepless nights worrying over how to pay the bills.

Buying more than you can afford is an easy trap to fall into. A cautious approach to shopping, like the one I learned from my mother, is one way to keep out of trouble.

And, if you think trouble can come from buying a pricey sweater—or even a pricey house—that you can't afford, imagine the trouble one could find themselves in if they bought five homes they couldn't afford.

Yes, I had some clients who did exactly that! This couple told me they had very big plans to up their income by investing in rental properties. They went big. They bought five homes. Their monthly mortgage payments were more than $6,000 a month.

What was their monthly income? $6,000 a month. They had taken on mortgage obligations that exceeded their income—and that was before all their other expenses were factored in.

How did they expect it to work? They figured it wouldn't be a problem because they would earn money by renting out the homes. It's never quite so simple.

"What if you never get them rented?" I asked. "You realize you're still responsible for the mortgage payments, right?"

They hadn't considered this or the possibility that, at any given time, one or more of the properties could need major repairs.

I asked another question. "Do you understand that if something goes wrong with any of the houses, you're responsible for paying to fix it?"

I could tell I was getting into areas they wished they'd thought about.

The truth is, it's typical to make zero profit on investments like this for up to five years. Mortgages are major obligations. While they stay steady, rents go up over time. That's when you'll start to make money in real estate—if you have the money to get started and the wherewithal to stick with it.

This is an argument for piece-by-piece real-estate investing—as your income can support the costs and you first learn the tricks of the trade. It's certainly not an argument for buying five houses right out of the gate, without the slightest idea of the costs involved.

To some degree, this intelligent couple was misled by the mortgage company. They assumed that since the loans were approved, they must be in a position to handle the costs. In hindsight, I'm sure they wish they'd worked out the numbers on their own first.

You're motivated, now what?

When you're psychologically motivated and ready to start saving and investing, there are all kinds of ways to make it happen.

A recent pharmacy-school graduate came to me with $125,000 in student loan debt. She really wanted to get rid of it. She decided to live at home for a year and pour all her income into retiring the debt. She was single, responsible for no one else, and determined. She managed to put $50,000 toward the debt in the first year—nearly half of what she owed! This put her into a position to pay off the rest in one-to-three years, depending on how she prioritized. She wasn't wasting any time paying off her debt so she could start planning for and funding her future.

You don't want to move in with your parents? Not a problem. There are plenty of other ways to fund your investments.

What if you could save $300 a month on car payments? That's the difference between buying a new car and a car that's two years old. That gives you an extra $300 a month you can funnel into your retirement.

Sure, it's nice to get a new car with that new-car smell and no miles on the odometer! You can drive it around and impress everyone (well, almost everyone—not financial planners).

Psychologically, it feels gratifying to walk into the car dealership and buy from the new-car department rather than the used-car department. I get it. But is the value you're getting really that much better? Most cars don't show significant wear and tear until they're four or five years old. Most don't break down until they're close to 10 years old—if that. Some of the higher-end brands can run like a dream for 15 years or more.

How many other decisions like this can you make? Can you cut your restaurant meals by half? Can you buy your toilet paper and paper towels at a discount store? These things add up, and they just require some good decisions and a little discipline. We're talking about things anyone can do. It's just a matter of whether you want to. If the rewards of the future serve as sufficient motivation, you'll master the discipline to make them happen.

Without motivation, there is no reward.

A couple came to me wanting a long-term financial plan. Yet, even with a plan, they continually spent all their income on sports equipment, exotic vacations, and the like. They spent money like crazy.

I told them to come back and see me when they'd saved $10,000. They never came back. I see them around occasionally. They still don't have any money saved. This couple absolutely could have done smart things that would have allowed them to save and invest, but they didn't want to.

We all have objectives—and they have theirs. This is their choice, for now anyway.

Seeing situations like this is not uncommon. People buy things, not because it's the smartest purchase or the best value, but because they decide they can somehow find the money to pay for it. Maybe it's a very expensive new truck. They want it so badly that they turn their budgets inside out until they can convince themselves they can afford the payments and not starve to death.

Will they have money left over to save or invest? No. Will they have money left over for an emergency? No. Will they be putting anything toward retirement? No.

But who cares? They've got a new truck!

One client spent her entire adult life pouring every cent of income beyond expenses into her kids. She will tell you today she has no regrets because her kids went to college, and now they are all happy in their careers.

I'm glad these kids did well with their college degrees. But financially, sending kids away to college when you don't really have the money—and they don't have a clear plan that college can help them execute successfully—isn't the best decision.

Another option would have been to let them enroll in community college for a year or two while living at home. They could have used that time to decide which career path they wanted to follow. It's not terribly expensive and wouldn't have put her on the hook for room and board, not to mention all the other ancillary costs of college.

In recent years, recognizing that college isn't for everyone is becoming more mainstream. That doesn't mean these kids aren't smart enough for college. It means that some kids' career paths are better pursued through trade schools, or internships, or entrepreneurships—or something else entirely.

You're not less smart if you skip college and pursue another path. You're less smart if you blow a bunch of money and time on college when you're not sure why you're doing it.

This particular client's kids did well after college, and I'm glad for them. But was this really the best scenario for her kids? Today, this client can't afford her own home and lives with one of her children. I'm sure her son loves his mother and is more than willing to take care of her. But it's far from clear that it was necessary—or the best decision—for her to forsake her own long-term goals in order to take care of her kids. Yet, people do this all the time.

Love your 60-year-old self.

You may be 30 today, but at some point, you're going to be 60. When you turn 60, do you want to look at your financial situation and ask yourself, "Dang it, what am I going to do?"

Surely, you would rather look at your financial situation and think, "Those decisions I made when I was 30 are really paying off now. My finances are in good shape."

The 30-year-old you should remember that the 60-year-old you is still you. Do that 60-year-old you a favor by tackling some of the things that are not really all that difficult now. When the 60-year-old you comes along, the consequences of failing to think, plan, or choose actions that could have set you up for the balance of your life, won't be an issue.

Get started on the path to financial security as soon as you can.

CHAPTER 3

Kids and Money: Setting Them on the Right Path Early

Technically, my job as a financial advisor is to manage people's portfolios. In reality, I often feel that I'm managing behaviors as much as anything else. That's because the behaviors you've learned throughout your life often shape how you think about and handle money. Kids are open books, eager to try new things. Having their own investing experiences at a young age will equip them with a positive outlook on money and make them confident investors as adults.

Home is the place to start.

The family finances are a good place to begin. They provide an enormous learning opportunity—one that shouldn't be missed.

When I was growing up in the 1970s, it was common for kids to know very little about the family's finances—perhaps it was a generational thing. Today's parents may have changed in this regard, but back in the day, "It's none of your business!" was a common refrain.

I'm sure there were reasons parents clung to this type of thinking. Perhaps they thought kids didn't have the capacity to understand family finances. Maybe they were afraid the kids would blab the details to their friends. Possibly, it was because the parents weren't doing well financially, and they were embarrassed to have the kids know. Whatever the reason, parents didn't seem to think the kids needed to know anything about the family's money situation. In some families, this is still true today, and it's a shame.

The perfect time to teach kids about household finance, saving, and investing is when they're young. There is no better environment than the home to teach kids what they need to know.

Home is personal.

It's easier to understand how household finances work because kids relate to what goes on in their own family. They eat the food that's purchased with the grocery money. They go on car trips that are paid for with the gas money. They live in the house that's paid for by the mortgage. They watch the shows that come through the Netflix subscription.

Teaching household finance with real examples is much more powerful than trying to communicate abstract ideas. Don't think they'll be interested? Tell them their cell phones will be in jeopardy if the family finances aren't in good shape. They'll pay attention.

Things cost money.

Many kids have skewed ideas about the things they have (and about the things they want) and where these things come from. Painting a realistic picture of the financial decisions your family makes can help kids make good choices throughout their lives.

A parent who works full-time is aware of the importance of every penny that goes toward paying for kids' clothing, school supplies, and sports equipment. Parents know what it took to earn that money. They know how much is left after everything is bought. Kids don't know these things. Kids have no idea what kind of budgeting is necessary to have these things without running out of money. They don't know—unless they're told.

Young minds are like sponges.

It's easier to shape psychological attitudes toward money at an early age. Money can bring about all sorts of feelings, such as fear, anxiety, apprehension, or greed. It can be seen as a problem, or it can also be seen as a resource that inspires strategic thinking and prompts thoughtful questions and interesting ideas. Once good attitudes and critical thinking are adopted, they are likely to stick through adulthood. Getting kids involved early is the best chance parents have of giving their kids a healthy and well-informed relationship with money—one they can carry with them throughout their lives.

The whole subject of money is less terrifying if you understand how it works. Let children gain an understanding of everything that happens and why it happens. Even the bumps in the road aren't as frightening if you understand that everybody has bumps, and that there are strategies to make you more resilient when the road is rough.

Many parents hesitate. Do they really want their kids to know how much they make? Do they want them to know how much they have in the bank? How about the monthly costs of running the household or the amount of their mortgage payment? Are you comfortable sharing these things with your kids? Before you say no, let's talk about Christmas. Yes, Christmas.

Do you really need a perfect Christmas?

In many families, a spectacular Christmas is an expectation. The house needs to look amazing—all dressed up in lights and glitter. Under the tree, there must be absolutely everything the kids could ever want, along with a few surprises. Christmas is the time when each member of the family, at least once, opens a gift that lights up their face with jubilation.

Christmas must be magical. Nothing less than that will do. This is the Christmas kids know and expect.

What they don't know is that their parents will pay the bills for that magical Christmas with a credit card that charges 18-percent interest. They don't know that the cost of this magic exceeded their parents' entire salary for the month of December. They don't know that it meant putting off the work that needed to be done on the family car so each of the kids could have that special present.

The reason they don't know these things is because they weren't told. They have no frame of reference. They probably understand, on some level, that their parents paid for the presents, but they don't have any idea how that impacts the family finances or the ability to take care of other priorities.

How is this state of blissful ignorance helping kids learn financial responsibility? How is it preparing them for the Christmases they'll have one day with their own kids? When should kids start learning about these things? When they're 18? When they're 25?

How about now!? Yes, now. This is your best opportunity—before they form ideas about money that have no relation to reality. Kids as young as 10 years old are not too young to learn these things. The family's own finances are the perfect place to start.

Good or bad, tell the whole truth.

How much should you tell them? Would your kids benefit from seeing a summary of your 401(k)? What if you explained the choices you make concerning it? You could then look up the annual report for each fund and explain the decisions that go into choosing which funds to buy. They'll learn how companies create value for investors, and because it's a 401(k) belonging to their own family, it will be real to them.

Explain your mutual funds—in simple terms, it's a basket of investments. Look over the annual report and the list of companies the mutual fund invests in and the number of shares they own. Recognizing some of the companies included may spark an interest.

Tell them about your struggles, too. How much did it set you back when your furnace went out? How did you deal with that situation?

What if your hours were cut at work, and you had to tighten your belt at home as a result? Tell them about it—in detail. Show them the reality of giving something up to save money. Let them experience it.

An unfortunate family situation unfolded recently when a father was laid off from his job. He and his wife didn't want their kids to know there was anything wrong. They said nothing and continued their usual spending patterns. They went out to eat and didn't cut back on any regular expenses.

Their kids were high school age. They were smart enough to realize their dad wasn't going to work, but their parents didn't talk to them about it. They didn't want to get them involved in their financial hardship.

Finally, when the parents came to me, their credit card balance had soared, and they weren't sure what to do.

We went through their budget and came up with a temporary strategy that would hold them over until the dad could get a new job. He proceeded to look for something more stable than the job from which he'd been laid off.

In the meantime, they missed a tremendous teaching opportunity. He was embarrassed about losing his job and decided it wasn't something the kids needed to hear about. As a result, his children were denied the opportunity to learn what happens when things don't go as planned. If they'd told their kids that money was tight, they could have all cut corners. They could have had a family discussion about the needed adjustments. They could have shown the kids the family budget and explained why changes were necessary.

But they didn't do that, and as a result, the kids didn't get to learn a life lesson.

As a parent, you might be uncomfortable discussing these things with your kids. But if you want them to do well in life financially, you'll do them a favor by being open and setting an example.

Doing the right things, opening up, and teaching your children about your finances are some of the most valuable gifts you can give them. You'll make it possible for them to grow up unafraid of money. They will be more likely to say, "Yes, I can do this!"

Set the stage.

Even very young kids can learn the basics of money management. They can understand spending (immediate gratification); they can understand saving for their goals (delayed gratification).

Here's an idea to get you started: Give them an allowance—maybe $1 per week, beginning at age 5. Put half of it into a "now jar" and the other half into a "later jar." They can spend what's in the "now jar" any time, but they can't touch anything in the "later jar" until it has $5 in it.

Human nature will have them wanting to go to a dollar store as soon as they have $1 in the "now jar." But once the "later jar" has the required $5, they might figure out they can get better stuff if they're patient. Some parents who have tried this told me their kids put everything into the "later jar" right away because they recognized this was the way to get a better value.

This is delayed gratification learned early! And it's one of the most powerful lessons a kid can learn.

Keep the conversation going.

As your kids get older, talk to them about the everyday decisions that impact the family's finances. Use examples they can relate to, such the cost of a dinner out at their favorite restaurant.

Let's say that dinner out for the entire family, including the tip, would cost $50. Preparing a perfectly good family meal at home would only cost $20.

How many times a week would the kids like to go out? Four? Okay, so how will it strike them to realize that by cutting back to once a week, you'd save the family $90 a week—or $360 a month?

Take it further. What if you show them that your mortgage costs the family $1,000 a month? That means that with the $360 you saved every month by eating at home, you'd have enough to pay four mortgage payments every year.

Will that make a difference to kids? It will if you show them that the family's savings account is $4,000 richer at the end of the year.

Now talk to them about the value of that $4,000 in terms of things they could buy, such as a TV or an Xbox. Talk about it in terms of a family vacation, or anything else they value.

You can also talk to them about it with a long-term view. For example, what will saving $4,000 a year beginning when you're 20 years old amount to when you're 60? $160,000 in just the principal—and that's before interest or investment returns!

If you just tell them to save money, but they don't understand what they can do with what they've saved, you'll have a harder time convincing them to forego the item they want to order online or that snack they want to buy right now. When they understand that money is an asset they can build into wealth—and that the power to do this is in their hands—they'll be on a path to financial prosperity.

Kids can be investors.

Okay, you've opened the door to your kids' financial futures with discussions about family finances. They are on the road to a healthy relationship with money. But responsible spending and saving money are only the tip of the iceberg. What if you open their young eyes to the world of investing? Yes, really! They can start when they're as young as 10 years old. And I don't mean they can start hearing about investing when they're 10 years old. I mean they can start investing.

My kids started at about that age, and they're still successfully investing as young adults. Here's how we began: I let them choose a company they liked, and they invested in it. We're not talking about thousands of dollars here; we're talking about a few hundred.

My son chose to buy Nintendo, and he did well with that investment. My daughter picked McDonald's, and that turned out to be an interesting experience. No sooner had she invested her money than mad cow disease reared its head and drove up the cost of beef. I told her what had happened and how it would affect McDonald's costs—and consequently their profits. She asked an interesting question that became another teaching opportunity.

"Why don't they just raise the price of hamburgers?" Great question—one that led to a discussion on competition, supply, and demand.

"Burger King, Wendy's, and Rally's aren't raising their prices," I said. "If McDonald's does, they'll lose customers." She didn't eat beef for a long time after that, but she did ride it out with her McDonald's investment.

Both kids chose their investments based on companies whose products they enjoyed. You might say that's not the most strategic approach to investing, but it was a great way to get them started and helped them learn the basics of how the market works.

Before they were teenagers, they were familiar enough with investing that it didn't scare them. They didn't see it as something for only rich people or Wall Street types. They understood that they, too, could invest.

When my daughter was 13, she bought shares of Apple. She invested only a few hundred dollars. By the time she was 28, her Apple shares were worth $13,000, and she sold them to come up with the down payment on her first home.

As a college freshman, she bought shares of Lululemon. A few months later, the stock skyrocketed after it was featured on Oprah. Her investment doubled. After a short discussion of whether to sell it all or keep it, she compromised and pulled out half of the value and reinvested in other stocks.

Around the same time, my son bought Under Armour stock. He's now looking into electrical supply companies because he deals with some of them at work, and he knows some good companies that he is willing to invest in.

They've had successes and setbacks. In the early 2000s, both became interested in the automotive industry. My son bought Ford stock, while my daughter invested in General Motors. The GM investment lost money when the company went through bankruptcy in 2009. Ford, on the other hand, weathered its way through that difficult period, helping my son prosper on an initial investment of $2 a share.

They learned to understand the trends of the market and knew not to fret about the ups and downs. When the market goes down, it's not time to panic; it's time to reinvest because shares are less expensive.

They also learned that investing is a long-term proposition. They didn't need a short-term gain. They could afford to wait, and that was exactly how I wanted them to think. It's helped them develop positive mindsets about money that will be with them for the rest of their lives.

Kids have purer minds than adults. Their brains haven't become encumbered with baggage that's born of negative experiences or bad influences. They can see investing as an opportunity and learn about how it can play a role in their lives.

Start small.

If your child starts investing before they are 18 years old, you can help them open a Uniform Transfer to Minors Act (UTMA) account. Your child's name will be on the account and you, or another adult, will be listed as the custodian. This account will be in your child's name and must be used for their purposes. An UTMA account can consist of stocks, mutual funds, or almost any type of investment.

Your child won't need a pile of money to get started. They'll only need an initial deposit of $250 for some funds. Then, they can add $50 thereafter, whenever they have the money. Nobody is going to call them to demand they invest more. They can start with their birthday money. Maybe you can offer to match them dollar for dollar, encouraging them to save more.

Don't be overly concerned about the taxes they'll owe on their gains. UTMA gains are taxed in tiers and there's no tax due on the first tier. The second tier is taxed at a child's rate which is typically lower than an adult's tax rate. If there are substantial gains, they may move to a third tier which is taxed at the parent's highest tax rate.

If they are older, have them sit down with you and an advisor to talk about their goals. Just like adults, kids should have a plan for their investments. Maybe they'll want to use their account earnings to save for their first car, college, or even a home. Reaching their goal will inspire them to continue on a healthy financial path throughout their lives.

Have the professional explain how investing works. Their UTMA will allow them to experience the ups and downs of the market at a young age. A professional can help them learn how to read an investment account and how to decipher an annual report so they can see for themselves how the companies that fund their purchases are doing. Maybe you'll learn something, too!

Ride out the storms.

One of the reasons I believe so strongly in teaching kids to invest is that, by having their own experience with investing, they'll be less likely to be influenced by the negative things they hear. And they will hear a lot of negative things.

Riding out the storms will help them see for themselves that, even when things look bleak, the market eventually bounces back.

Look at what happened in the early part of 2020, when the COVID-19 pandemic hit and the lockdowns began. The stock market, which had been soaring for several years, suddenly cratered. It wasn't surprising.

I tell people to hold their stocks when the market hits a rough patch, but people often sell. The inevitable spin from the news media is, "The market will never come back!" History says this notion is preposterous. Yet, people lack historical perspective and think every major negative event is unlike all that came before it. "Oh sure," they think. "Markets bounced back in the past, but nothing like this has ever happened before!"

We heard it in 2020, and we heard it back in 2008 after the mortgage market melted down. Both times, we were told that this was an extremely unique event—we wouldn't see recovery like we'd seen after other shocks to the system. But we did.

The predictions of market doom didn't originate in 2008, either. I'm reminded of a news report I saw in which we were told that international events were causing the market to crash, and that it would never come back. This was in 1972, as the oil crisis was starting.

In case you think we've experienced some extraordinary events lately, let me share some headlines with you:

1. *U.S. Budget Deficit Hits New High*
2. *Oil Prices Skyrocket 400%*
3. *Dow Closes At Lowest Level in More Than a Decade*
4. *Double-Digit Unemployment Fuels Fears*
5. *Persistent Job Woes Test Economy*
6. *Stock Market Meltdown*
7. *Polarized Politics: Is A Solution Possible?*
8. *Longest Government Shutdown In US History*

Sound familiar? These are all things that are currently happening, right? But the headlines aren't new at all. Here is the year in which each of them was published:

1. 1972; 2. 1973; 3. 1974; 4. 1982; 5. 1993; 6. 2008; 7. 2013; 8. 2018

People who didn't understand the nature of markets were spooked during these years. Many bailed on their stocks. But some were probably familiar with a thing called a mountain chart. I'm sure you've seen one, even if you don't know the term. It's a chart that shows the stock market's ups and downs over a period of time.

Here's one that shows the trends in the Standard and Poor's 500, from just before the onset of the Great Depression to the present day:

The gray strips represent the periods when the market was in decline. Otherwise, you see white as the background, and that represents times when the market was rising. There are 14 gray strips, and they correspond to events you probably remember. As you can see, the stock market crash of 1929 is the most significant. Then there are the recessions of 1991 and 2008, the 9/11 attacks of 2001, and the COVID-induced collapse of 2020.

Markets have their ups and downs. But when you look at the totality of the chart, what trend do you see? It's always more up than down.

So, if that's the case, why bail during a down time? History suggests the market will bounce back, so why not take that occasion to reinvest? Shares are less expensive, and you can get more value out of them over the long term.

And why would you believe news reports that imply all is lost because a momentary setback has driven down prices? There are no cataclysmic events that have permanently crippled the market. The Great Depression didn't do it. No recession has done it. No war has done it. No terrorist attack has done it.

Stay in markets for the long haul, and don't overreact to isolated events. Don't be fooled by panicky analysts or shallow news reporting that drives so many to pull out their investments. Markets outlive moments in time because people will always come back to look for ways to build businesses and build wealth, and they will always need capital.

Be a good example.

Parents don't always do a good job setting financial examples for their kids. If they don't have control over their own financial lives, it can look like utter chaos to their kids. There might be piles of paper everywhere, with no sense of organization. Often, there are far too many bank accounts, of which no one knows the purpose (let alone how much money is in them). Maybe there's a 401(k), but no one has a clue of its value.

I had a couple come to see me who fit this description. They brought their 12-year-old daughter with them. The longer we spent going through their disaster of unorganized papers and tracking where their money was, the more I noticed the daughter's growing frustration.

Finally, she asked, "Mom and Dad, how did you let this get so bad?"

Believe it or not, this was a hopeful sign.

She observed her parents' financial situation and didn't think this was the norm. She understood that they could have—and should have—done better. I paid attention and made sure that during the rest of the time they were there, she had the opportunity to learn from their mistakes. Maybe it will result in better habits for her in her own adult life.

Then, there's the example set by the "we-made-it" type couples. They make it look like money's easy to come by and that there's no limit to what you can spend. They give their kids what they want, when they want it. I'm sure they think it's a form of love. However, the kids aren't learning anything about how hard one needs to work to earn money or how smart you need to be to keep it.

I had one such couple come to see me. Their kids felt quite entitled. They expected new cars when they turned 16, and they got them. They expected the latest clothes, the latest technology—you name it. They expected to get it, and generally, they did.

If they'd had to work for some of this, or at least understood the sacrifices necessary to get it, this might not have been a total loss. But the parents hadn't taught them any of this. They just collected large paychecks and spent the money freely on everything their children wanted.

They finally came to me when they realized it was catching up with them. They were getting to the age where they knew they should start thinking about retirement, and they didn't have a clue—let alone a plan.

As we went through their various accounts, I showed them how much money they needed to apply toward retirement savings. The wife cried. Her husband sat there, unable to understand what had happened.

"We work so hard for our money!" she said. "We have nothing to show for it."

They needed to make a lot of changes to the way they were living, and the hardest part would be the push-back they would get from their children. In their children's eyes, there would be no apparent reason to stop getting everything they wanted. Their parents had the same jobs. They made the same money. So, what was the problem?

The problem was that the parents were finally looking toward the future and were realizing they hadn't put themselves into a good position. They'd accumulated a lot of stuff, but no wealth to build on. Things needed to change, and the kids weren't going to like it one bit.

If the parents were willing to explain exactly what happened and why these changes were necessary, it might serve as the wake-up call that allowed the kids to avoid the same mistakes when they became adults. It would be a difficult cycle to break, however. The spend-happy mindset had already been established.

Setting a good example doesn't have to be anything big. Even small choices can serve as examples. I know of a family with four kids that likes to go out to eat. When they go out, they only order waters to drink. They are millionaires, they can afford to buy sodas. But they know that sticking with waters saves them $12 to $15 per meal. They're establishing an important principle for their kids. "Don't blatantly drop money on something you don't really need when another option, which is free, is perfectly sufficient." They're teaching their kids to spend money only when they're going to get value back in return, and to learn to live with small sacrifices if it means building more wealth.

.I had another client with two daughters. Every time something around his house needed to be fixed, he asked one of his daughters to get the tools and help him. It didn't matter what it was, from the toilet to the garbage disposal, the daughters were involved in fixing it.

What's the point of this story? By the time the girls were grown, they were self-sufficient in the upkeep of their own homes. Their dad didn't just fix everything himself. He used it as a teaching opportunity.

Even unfortunate choices can be teaching moments. Did you feel that you absolutely had to have a brand-new car only to realize after six months, when it didn't feel so new anymore, you would have been better off buying a slightly used car? It wasn't a good choice. Tell your kids how much money that decision cost. They can learn from it.

Maybe you made the same mistake with the house you bought. The kids might love the big house, but it would be an eye-opener to show them how much financial pressure it put on you and the things you had to do to deal with that pressure. Admitting to making mistakes is setting as good an example as doing the right thing upfront.

They're growing up!

A first job is more than just a chance to earn some pocket money. It's an introduction to adulthood.

When my kids were teenagers, I decided it was time for them to get jobs—beyond babysitting and odd jobs. It was time to go to an employer and learn how to apply and interview for a job.

I was surprised by their hesitation and lack of confidence. This was a scary venture for them, but I coached them through the process.

Even when their apprehension looked like annoyance and unreceptiveness, I used my "mom voice" to keep them on track. By the third or fourth request for an application, their attitudes improved.

I gave them very detailed and literal instructions.

"Go into the restaurant and ask for an application. Come back to the car to fill it out. Copy down your references. Go inside and give it to the manager or ask for the manager's name and phone number. Write it down!"

Sound ridiculous? It was, but it was necessary. They didn't know how to do this.

You can do the same for your teens. No matter what job they seek, explain that they must show the company who they are and how valuable they will be to the organization. This will take them into adulthood and help them become an employee who is sought after—whether it's a desk job, construction job, or sales job. They'll profit by understanding the process and by learning how they can add value to an organization.

When they get a job, listen to your kids' observations about it. Be open to conversations about their bosses and coworkers. What do they like about it? What is their least favorite part? These observations could help them decide the direction of their future career. And hopefully, it will match up with the school subjects they like best, too.

A lot of kids who go to college still aren't sure of their goals or why they're there. To help them, find out what careers they're considering. Help them find people in those fields they can job-shadow for a day or two. Is there a friend or family member in the field? Can they reach out to someone on LinkedIn? You never know who might be willing to mentor a young person. There are many opportunities, but you might have to help by giving them a nudge in the right direction.

Even after college graduation, your kids will benefit by having you as their coach and cheerleader. Help them practice interviewing for jobs. My husband and I gave our kids some hard questions that we thought they might be asked at an interview and guided them to come up with answers. They looked up the companies where they were interviewing. They learned who the company's customers were. They learned who the person was who would be interviewing them. Interviews are hard! Your teens will appreciate that you're there to support them and soon, they'll be ready to go out there and tackle the world!

CHAPTER 4

It's Not Gambling

A client called, brimming with excitement because a friend had turned her on to a "hot stock." One single "hot stock."

As financial advisors, we employ all kinds of strategies based on clients' objectives and risk tolerance. We build diversified portfolios across asset classes. We don't chase "hot stocks." But the client insisted.

"Do we have any information about this stock?" I asked.

"No," she said. But she trusted the friend.

Under protest, we bought the stock. It took a month for it to lose half its value. The loss would not have been as severe if her portfolio was diversified with hundreds of companies versus only this one stock. Maybe it would come back, but it's a risk. Not long after that, the client stated the obvious, "I should have listened to you."

Since then, we've had this client in a strategic investment plan that follows the long-term trends of the market, and she doesn't jump at "hot stocks" or momentary attractions anymore.

Stay calm and be patient.

Too many people think the market is like gambling, or that making money in the market is about inside information you get before anyone else. It's not, but people see it portrayed like that in movies, on TV shows, and in news reports.

Sometimes, strong emotions send inexperienced investors in the other direction. During a recent downturn in the market, a client called in a panic. She wanted out. She spent a half hour insisting that she wanted out now, even as I explained to her that markets would bounce back with time. I told her that her best move would be to buy more shares because the prices were low. "Look at the downturns as an opportunity, not as something to fear," I rationalized.

Finally, she calmed down.

But her calmness was temporary. Soon, she called back. Once again, she was in a panic. She had probably read more financial news on the internet or watched some TV show with "investing experts" talking about the doom that awaited all investors.

"It's my decision, and I want to sell!" she informed me.

It was clear that I could continue to explain the logic of staying in the market, but her fear and panic were not going to subside. It didn't matter that the facts were on my side. I wasn't going to convince her. Against my better judgment, we sold her shares.

You can probably imagine the conversation we had some months later when the market was once again heading in a positive direction, and she realized how much money she would have made if she had taken my advice.

"Why did you let me sell?" she asked.

A lot of my job is human psychology and managing investment behavior—often a bigger part than the financial strategies. The finance part takes knowledge, experience, and skill. But, in many ways, markets can be more predictable and rational than people. It all goes back to the ways they've learned to think about money over the course of their lives.

Think positive.

Money is emotional for people. I get that. It's a source of worry and fear because the consequences of losing it are severe. That doesn't mean you're going to help yourself by panicking over things that are out of your control, or when you let fear undermine common-sense strategies.

It's hard, but negative attitudes can be changed. With some thought, you may even figure out where your negative attitude toward money originated. Understanding this might help you turn away from the "I'm going to lose" pattern of thinking and, instead, think in terms of long-term gains. With experience, time, and patience—and by surrounding yourself with positive people—you can gain a positive attitude toward money.

It is interesting when I talk with someone who invested during the financial crisis of 2008—or any crash for that matter. Some say they lost money, and it was the worst thing ever. Others say they waited it out, or took advantage of the low market to invest more. Others just kept investing and ignored the news; they didn't need their money right away. Their investment was for retirement, and they were looking for long-term results. They kept investing, stayed on track, and hardly paid attention to the news of the day.

When I talk to the people who pulled their money out and lost, I bluntly ask them if they needed the money right then. Unless they also lost their jobs during that time, most say they didn't and admit that they regret their decision. Recognizing this is key, and will hopefully inspire a different reaction next time.

During the 2020 election season, a lot of clients were on edge because of the way news was reported. The market would be up one day because the polls swung in a certain direction, the news of a COVID-19 vaccine sounded encouraging, or the economic recovery news sounded good. Then, the market would be down on another day because COVID-19 cases were rising, or this or that candidate had done poorly in a debate.

It would have been smart for some clients to shut off the news entirely—or, at the very least, separate it from their investing decisions. Shutting out the noise doesn't come naturally to people. As a financial planner, much of my job is persuading people to hang in there even when they think they want out. Successful investing often means doing the opposite of what you're feeling.

No one knows what the market is going to do at any point in time. Anyone who tells you they do is lying. Timing the market almost never works. In fact, this approach heightens your risks. There's a much greater chance that you'll make nothing on your investment and, instead, lose a lot. That's a risk there is no reason to take.

So, what techniques work? Investing something every single month—automatically and systematically. Let a portion of your income flow directly into your investments—even before you see it. Teach yourself to live off only the remaining income.

People who hang in through the highs and lows almost always do well in the long term. They don't subject themselves to high-risk or panicky moves. It's almost a no-brainer, so why would anyone take a different approach? It's because of how they think about money. They need to learn to look at it a new and better way.

Create a plan, step-by-step.

Let's just say you have $500 more income each month than expenses. What do you do with that $500? How do you develop a plan? First, it's important that you know why you're doing what you're doing. The answers to these three questions will help you get started:

1. What are you saving for?

2. How much time do you have?

3. How much risk are you willing to accept?

Don't forget that before you consider investing that $500 in pursuit of a big return, you need to have enough cash set aside for emergencies. It's boring, but if you don't have three-to-four months' worth of income saved to cover an emergency, deposit that $500 in the bank and collect whatever interest you get. If, however, you've got those emergencies covered, move ahead!

What are you saving for?

You're not going to achieve your goals if you don't know what they are and why you're pursuing them. Are you determined to save for a comfortable retirement, but you also want to buy a house? Will you need a car in the near future? Knowing your goals helps determine your strategy.

How much time do you have?

How much time do you have to accomplish your goals? If you're focusing on retirement, and it's 10 or more years away, that gives you options. You won't need the full amount you've saved all at once. If your investments are sound and you're able to save enough, you can take a check from the earnings every month and have a reliable monthly income. Whether the amount in the funds goes up or down, you'll still get your monthly check.

Why do I use "10 years or more" as the marker? Here's a historical tidbit: In the history of the market, starting in 1926, there has only been one time that a 10-year period ended with total value of the market down. Check for yourself. Pick any point in the market's history and go forward 10 years from that point. The market will have made money every time except for this one instance.

Sure, there have been momentary glitches within those 10-year periods. But there's never been a glitch that's lasted so long, or been so severe, that it caused the overall 10-year period to end up in the negative forever.

If you are scrutinizing this one single loss, then you're missing the point. Keeping a long-term perspective is what counts. It's also worth mentioning that most portfolios are not 100% Standard and Poor's 500 (S&P 500) stocks. Portfolios are made up of a balance of different types of investments with different levels of risk. There are no guarantees, but diversification may provide better returns with less risk over time.

Don't fret over current events. Often, people get caught up in the drama of politics and the effect they fear it will have on their investments. According to a recent American Funds study, however, it's not a major influencer of the market. It doesn't even matter who wins elections. Markets have performed similarly, regardless of who is in office. Over the long term, they've consistently gone up.

What does all of this mean for you? If you have 10 years or more, you can put your money in a growth fund and call it a day. If the ups and downs make you nervous, then for your own peace of mind, don't even look at it. You'll get a nice start on a pot of money to help fund your retirement and to recreate the income you'll need.

What if your goal is less than 10 years away?

Maybe you're thinking about goals that aren't so far in the future—like buying a car, for instance. Granted, you could just finance it. Many people do. They borrow a large amount of the purchase price and make payments with interest over the course of several years.

But what if you did it the opposite way? What if you put money away for several years before buying a car? During that time, you'd collect interest instead of paying interest. Then, when you bought it, you could pay with cash and it would be yours, free and clear.

So, you want to buy a car in five years? Determine how much money you'll need to save during that period. If the car costs $10,000, then you need to put aside just under $200 a month to accumulate $10,000 over five years. You'll probably earn interest, of course, but let's plan for just the principle and consider the interest a bonus. Then, once you've got the car, you can shift that $200 a month to your retirement fund.

The key is to consistently put the money into each fund every month and get used to living on what you have left over. If you do this every month—regardless of whether the market is up, down, left, or right—you'll realize that the gains are available for you when you need them.

How much risk are you willing to accept?

Putting money in the bank versus investing it is a choice. Let's look at the difference, using $20,000. The bank may pay you 0.25 percent, or $50 per year. You can do this, or you can invest this money and potentially earn much more.

Even an average of a 2-percent return would be $400 per year. You'd be making the choice to risk your money knowing that the market fluctuates. If you have enough emergency money in the bank, you can afford to invest the $20,000 for more potential gain. And, since you have emergency money set aside, you can take the time to wait out the fluctuations of the market. These are the rewards for taking the calculated risk.

Do you see how your way of thinking is changing? You're no longer reactive, but proactive and strategic. You're no longer panicky about money. Instead, you're learning to apply it as an asset and a resource. You're no longer wondering how you'll do the things you want to do. You're taking charge and making it happen. You're no longer afraid of making a big mistake. You are remaining systematic and committed to your plan.

This is how everyone could think about money. It's just a matter of paying attention and understanding what to do with the resources you have.

Procrastination has a price.

Starting sooner is always better, even if you put away a smaller amount. There's a huge cost to waiting until later. Take this story about two cousins as an example.

One cousin started saving early. She saved $600 a month for 20 years. Based on an 8-percent return, her retirement withdrawals amounted to $1,187 per month in income.

The second cousin waited 10 years before he started saving. He figured he'd catch up by saving twice as much. So, once he got started, he put away $1,200 a month for 10 years. But he couldn't catch up this way because the first cousin's money had already been working for her for 10 years, earning another 8% each year before he even got started. And the earnings were earning 8% right along with her annual investments. When it was time for him to retire, even at the same interest rate of 8 percent, his withdrawals only generated an income of $741 a month.

Let's look at it again, just to be sure it's clear.

Save now:
- $600/month for 20 years at 8% average return
- 4% withdrawals from investment = $1,187/month

Save later:
- $1200/month for 10 years at 8% average return
- 4% withdrawals from investment = $741/month

The cost of waiting is impossible to ignore. Invest now with whatever money you can afford to put toward the effort.

Maybe you feel like you don't have a dime to spare. You probably do, though; you just need to know where to look. Most people have cash-flow leaks and, once the leaks are plugged, the extra amount can be invested. Here are just a few examples:

- Shop around for a better homeowners or auto insurance rate.
- Cancel credit cards that have annual fees.
- Cancel auto-payments for the gym membership you haven't used in months.
- Contact your cable/internet provider to see about a better rate.

How many things like this could you do? How much money would that free up to channel into investments? There are always places to find cash if it's important enough to you.

Pay attention to your finances.

Lots of people are oblivious to their finances, and it costs them—now and in the long run. When I prepare summaries for clients that show them exactly where their money is going, it's often a revelation. They've never seen their finances summed up so comprehensively. And they've certainly never considered tracking them so closely.

The summary includes a list of all assets, both where they are now and where they should be at the time of retirement. It also shows total debt and a protection area that lists life, health, and disability insurances. Everything is summed up on about two pages, right there in front of them.

It is easy to follow—and very telling.

I once met with a couple at their home. They were raising two children and were both very intelligent engineers. Their desk was littered with piles and piles of papers—all financial information. They had no idea what most of it was or what to do with it. They had never even looked at most of the documents.

I asked how much their assets were earning. They had no idea.

I asked about their 401(k). They told me they weren't sure where in the market it had been invested. It turned out it wasn't in the market at all. It was in cash. They hadn't known that either.

Another client was a business owner. I asked how much money his company earned on a quarterly basis, and how he was investing the earnings. He didn't know the answer to the first, which left the second largely moot.

People should have a good sense of what's going on in their financial lives. They may struggle to understand small-cap international funds, but they can still become familiar with the categories in which their 401(k) funds are invested. They can be helped by working with a qualified financial advisor.

There's help available.

I am very grateful for the fact that my first degree is in psychology. It has been very useful in serving my clients. I appreciate that it is stressful to invest when you do not know what to expect. I counsel clients to be comfortable with being uncomfortable. Our meetings often turn into personal discussions about issues and concerns—sometimes this, rather than their investment performance or asset classes, turns out to be the focus of the meeting.

They come in to discuss whether they should buy a cottage, update their kitchen, or buy a car. They want to explore how this will affect their plans and other goals. Sometimes, we will discuss an issue for an hour or two. It's well worth the time if it allows them to be comfortable with the adjustments they'll have to make to achieve their goals.

You don't have to be trained as a chief financial officer to know how to make good decisions with money. If you find yourself with a little extra money at the end of the month, what would you do with it? If you've got your financial priorities and goals defined, it should be an easy call. Maybe you'd put a third in the bank, a third in an intermediate fund, and a third in an IRA. You simply align your decision with your goals.

This is a good system for kids, too. A few years back, some clients had kids who had gotten a bunch of money for their bar mitzvahs. They wanted to make good decisions about what to do with the money.

I explained to them that they could take a balanced approach by putting some of it in a bond and some of it in a growth fund. It was a great learning experience for them. The bond was much more stable and didn't go up and down like the growth fund did. When the market was up, they saw half their money aggressively rising while the other half was steady and boring and didn't really move much.

When the growth fund went down, they saw the bonds as an anchor to them.

This worked because it was a good plan, but it also worked because the kids valued saving money. They wanted to learn, and they were open to good advice. They are still learning and still doing well with their money today.

You earned it, you saved it, but then…

Convincing people to save and invest can be difficult. Even when it looks like they're headed down the right path, things come along in life that derail good habits and deplete hard-earned savings.

Weddings are a big offender.

I have seen women pay $5,000 for a dress they're going to wear for one day. I understand that it's a big day, but come on. This makes no sense, especially when you can buy used dresses that look fantastic for much less.

It doesn't stop there. It seems every wedding needs to be a day that leaves each guest in awe. There must be an ice sculpture (add another $2,000 to the bill)! You need to have a live band, an open bar, gift bags with iPhones—it's insane. Couples could buy cars or, in some cases, homes with what they spend on this extravagance.

What if they saved the money ahead of time so they could pay for their wedding with cash? Does that make it okay? Well, it's their money. But if they'd been a little more humble when making their wedding plans and put the money into investments instead, they could have watched it grow into more money.

One of the best weddings I've attended was a potluck at a park. Someone manned the barbecue and prepared burgers and hot dogs. It wasn't fancy, but kids played happily, adults socialized, and the couple streamed a playlist of their favorite music. My family had a wonderful time. We didn't judge the event based on how much money was spent. Families and friends were brought together to celebrate this couple's special occasion. I bet if you look back, you'll also find that some of the best times you've had weren't elaborate, high-cost affairs. The emotional bonds and the quality time you spent together was much more important. We need to think about money in a logical and practical way. Do you really need to spend a pile of money to achieve your goals?

Cars can be another financial enemy. I had a client who wanted to get started saving money. Then, he went out and spent $70,000 on a souped-up pickup truck. That truck had everything—every factory option and lots of accessories. That truck was his priority, and he got what he wanted. It was his call, not mine. But he had a wife, and that $70,000 was money he didn't have to leave for her if something happened to him.

Let me tell you about another client.

A woman came to see me—widowed and terrified. Her husband had just died from a sudden car accident. He had always handled the bills and all their finances. She hadn't worked full-time in years and was looking for help figuring out where she could find a job and what she would have to earn to make ends meet.

Before he passed, the couple had met with me regularly about their financial plan. They had things in good order and worked as a team. The husband took charge of paying the bills and handling the finances, in general, and the wife took care of everything else.

She was involved, but mainly just to listen and be part of the conversation. She was not totally in the dark, but this wasn't her wheelhouse. When her husband died, the finances were scary and overwhelming.

I suggested that we look at the arrangements her husband had made before he passed away. We did. And she was amazed.

The entire time they'd been married, he'd been putting away money. He knew when one of them passed, the other would need an income of about $5,000 a month to maintain the lifestyle they were used to. And he had saved enough money that she'd be able to draw that amount monthly from the fund.

"The investments and interest will recreate the income your husband was bringing in," I explained to her. "You're fine. You don't have to get a job if you don't want one."

She cried. She had no idea he'd prepared so well. He went to great lengths to take care of her before he died. That was a true sign of his love for her.

Of course, since she knew so little about her finances, we needed to spend a considerable amount of time going over them. We spent about 12 hours in meetings helping her understand everything—his life insurance, his pension, the whole picture.

He had prioritized their well-being over things like trucks, ice sculptures, and other indulgences.

People tell me they don't know where to find the time to manage their finances. I ask them how many hours they spend each week at work. Most say it's around 40 to 50 hours. I ask them if they could find half an hour, maybe at the end of one workday or on a Saturday, to tend to their finances. None can tell me with a straight face that they can't come up with that. You can do it if it's important enough to you—and it should be important enough to everyone.

What are your assets?

I teach a financial management class at a local university. One of the first questions I ask students is, "What is an income-producing asset?"

The students come up with some interesting answers. A car is a common one. They figure that they own it, it has market value, so it's an asset.

Then, I ask them how much money their car produces for them.

"Oh."

Then, someone will usually suggest, "A home."

I ask, "Is your home producing income for you?"

"Hmm."

These are possessions, not income-producing assets (also known as wealth-producing assets). Often, people don't understand the difference. Just because something is a possession, and theoretically could be sold for a certain amount of money, doesn't mean it's a wealth-producing asset. Obviously, we all need a place to live, and we need a way to get around. But just because you spend money on these things, doesn't mean you should consider them assets.

A wealth-producing asset is one that can make you money. Stocks and bonds are this type of asset. They can produce money. Invest in stocks and bonds instead of accumulating possessions that don't produce wealth.

Is your house an investment?

A home is a good way to build equity, but many people think of their home as more than just a place to live—an investment. They think they'll sell it when they retire and live off the money. But really? Then where will they live? Another home will also cost money and they won't come out ahead unless they downsize considerably.

If a home is paid off before retirement, it is a secure place to live without the risk of rent increases. Buy a home with this in mind, and buy within your means. Consider the taxes, home insurance, utilities, lawn care, landscaping, painting, furnishings, and have a plan for unexpected repairs. If costs are underestimated, you could be forced to sell or lose the home to foreclosure. When commissions and the costs of moving are considered, you've lost a bundle in the deal.

Also, think twice about taking out that home-equity loan. These loans are sometimes looked at as if they were a bank account. Need a new car? Do you want to take a vacation or a take on a home renovation? Great! Just take out a home equity loan! But wait! It's not that easy. There are many fees and costs that go along with borrowing money from the equity in your home. You will do yourself a favor by first saving money in an account or intermediate portfolio that is specified for your goals, rather than borrowing.

A home could be considered an investment if you're buying the home to rent out or flip—and it won't be where you live. This would be a long-term investment, just like mutual funds. But before you buy that investment property, look at the big picture first. For a flip, you'll need a down payment. You'll need to pay the taxes and utilities while you are fixing it up. And you'll need to have the means to fund the renovation. If all goes as planned, you'll make a profit when you sell—especially if you're ready to put in the many hours of labor it will take. Your profits will be less if you need to pay professionals for the work, but hopefully, you'll still earn enough for the down payment on your next flip.

With a rental home, the income from rent typically covers only the mortgage and expenses. Breaking even is a good goal for the first 5 years or so. After 5 or

10 years, when the home has built up some equity, you can refinance (yes, that costs money, too!). Then, the income from the rent will more easily cover the lower mortgage payment, the expenses, and the upkeep and you can begin to see some profit.

I can tell you from my own experiences that being a landlord is a lot of work. You'll want to think of it as a part-time job—keeping the books, taking care of the maintenance, and managing renters. It's challenging. With my properties, it always seemed that I was out of town when something went wrong, and I found myself scrambling to find the right professional. Have a database of good resources on hand—it's a must!

So, is it starting to make sense? The home you live in is a place to live, not an investment. But what if you pay the house off and sell it? Can you turn it into a wealth-producing asset that way? Probably not. Let's say you buy a house for $200,000 and make payments on the mortgage for 30 years. The interest and taxes will result in well over $300,000 in payments. Then, you turn around and sell it after 30 years for twice what you paid for it. That's $400,000. You didn't even get back what you paid in interest and taxes alone. It's a nice chunk of change, but you still lost money on the deal over the course of 30 years. And that's before you consider the cost of upkeep and home improvements. Your home is simply not an income-producing asset.

Cars are an even worse investment. They always depreciate, and no one ever sells one for more than they bought it for—even if it's kept it in great condition. The longer you keep it, the more expensive it becomes. Warranties expire and things start to give way. Face it, cars and houses aren't assets that are meant to produce income.

Then, what IS an investment?

Stocks and bonds are assets intended to be used to produce income one day or grow while you are accumulating wealth. The market value of stocks and bonds will fluctuate, but they will never lose the ability to produce wealth. They won't cost money in the same way possessions do—unless, of course, you panic and sell them when their prices are down.

Annuities are also assets, albeit ones that are not well understood by many. Think of them as something like a pension. Their purpose is to produce a regular monthly income. They're often purchased with a significant lump sum of money, perhaps from a life insurance payout or an inheritance. Sometimes they're purchased with a lump sum from a 401(k) or an IRA at retirement.

Here's how they work. Let's say that you receive an inheritance of $100,000. An investment advisor might ask you to determine the amount of monthly income you'll need to live on when you retire. If it's more than you currently have, they might recommend your inheritance money be put into an annuity that will generate monthly payments for you when you retire.

By buying an annuity, you're giving up your lump sum of $100,000 in exchange for, say, $350 a month. You're not going to take the risk of putting that $100,000 in stocks and watching it grow. You're simply going to lock it in and draw the monthly income it produces for you when you retire, like receiving a pension. In fact, those who retire with a pension are sometimes offered the choice of a monthly income or receiving a lump sum—which they could use to purchase an annuity.

Annuities get a bad reputation in the market, because they're often misunderstood. Most retirees desire and need some guaranteed income. Would I rather see young people be more aggressive and invest the money in growth funds since they have more time? Sure. But if the risks would keep them awake at night, I'm not doing anyone any favors by arm-twisting. The guarantee of an annuity works for some people. It meets their needs and it's a fit for their mindset.

Here's what it boils down to: You can invest your money with no guarantees but gain flexibility and an opportunity for more growth; or, you can choose a product that guarantees income for the rest of your life but has no flexibility and no opportunity for growth.

Or, you can do both. Split your money. Put part of it in a guaranteed annuity, and put the rest into investments. Find a comfortable combination that works for you.

Understand that the more time you have, the less risk you're taking when choosing stocks and bonds. Let's look at the results from an ICA fund over different periods of time to illustrate the point:

American Funds Investment Company of America (ICA) Fund Performance results since fund's establishment in 1934				
	Positive Returns	Negative Returns	% Positive	% Negative
One year:	58	29	67%	33%
Three years:	74	11	87%	13%
Five years:	77	6	93%	7%
Ten years:	78	0	100%	0%

This is a chart of an American Funds ICA Fund, and its performance over 1-, 3-, 5- and 10-year periods since the fund began in Detroit in 1934. You will notice that the longer you wait, the more likely you will have a positive return on your investment. For instance, over 78 10-year periods, this fund made money 100% of the time, whereas, the 87 one year periods show that it made a positive return 58 times and a negative return 29 times. Note that this fund is made up of stocks only.

Granted, this is just one fund. Others will perform differently, but this is a great example of the benefit of giving yourself more time to weather fluctuations and to take advantage of the longer-term, upward trend in the market. The longer you keep an investment, the more likely it is you will have better results.

Three tips to help you become a better investor.

1. **Accept declines as a normal part of the investment cycle.** They're natural and temporary, so don't let them fill you with dread or panic. History has shown declines to be inevitable, but it has also shown that the market has recovered.

2. **Long-term perspective is important.** Don't place too much emphasis on recent events, even during a downturn. Remember, stocks reward investors over time. You're in it for the long haul.

3. **Don't try to time the market.** Losses can feel twice as bad as gains feel good, but stand your ground when the market is down. Selling during a downturn will lock in your losses, and you'll miss out on the gains when the market recovers.

Listen, learn, and do it!

The best thing you can do for your future is to go into your adult life with a healthy attitude about money. Understand what wealth-producing assets are. Invest steadily and consistently regardless of the twists and turns of the market. Don't be frightened by the little blips that cause the market to momentarily decline. Learn to turn money into a productive asset that gives you peace of mind and resources for your future.

If you're further on in life and haven't saved, invested, or overcome the fear of finances—there are choices. Annuities may not have the wealth-producing potential of growth-oriented investment funds, but they do produce a guaranteed income. Remember, doing something now is always better than doing nothing.

Master these concepts and discipline yourself. Put away substantial savings and recreate a sizable income for your future self. Shed bad habits, embrace better ones. Do all of this as early in life as possible. Don't be afraid.

Listen, learn, and do it.

"Every young person, no matter the disadvantages they face, can aspire to do better. All they need is a good mentor, some wise direction, and the right opportunities to learn and grow."

—*Jill Gleba*

CHAPTER 5

Careers:
Finding Your Place

Although this chapter discusses teens and how parents can help them find a suitable career, it's not only for young people. The advice in this chapter can be for you at any age. Whether you are searching for your place in the work world or thinking of changing careers, I hope you will find some help and inspiration here.

Do you think most kids know what kind of career they want when they're 10 years old? How about when they're 13…or 16?

Some do, but most don't. They're trying to get through school, and are dealing with the growing pains of being a kid. But maybe they'd think more about it if they were prompted to do so by the adults in their lives.

They're told to get good grades and finish school. Then it's time to get into college and do well there. Education is valuable, of course! But when we think about the pursuit of education, we often lose sight of the fact that it should lead to something.

Fortunately, kids don't have to decide to commit their entire lives to a certain career when they're 10 years old—or even when they're 18. People change their minds all the time as they learn, grow, and experience life. But the teenage years—or even pre-teen years—are a great time to get them thinking about what interests them and what they might like to pursue in their lives.

How do they decide?

When choosing a career, how do kids know they're making the right choice? What if they could see it in action—in real life? Wouldn't that give them a much better idea of whether a certain job might be right for them? Sometimes, companies have job-shadowing programs for exactly this purpose. They invite young people to spend a day observing and experiencing their profession. If your kids can find a company that offers an experience like this, encourage them to sign up. Can't find one? Have them reach out to someone in the field and ask if they can spend an hour or two with them to see what their job is like. They can start by asking neighbors or relatives about what they do. They can ask what they like and dislike about their jobs. What other careers might they have chosen based on their education and experience? You never know who might be able to help.

If they don't make any connections through family, friends, and neighbors, encourage them to look on LinkedIn. It's very easy to find people in any given field. Have them search for those with job titles that interest them and send connection requests. Once they've connected, have them pick out a person they'd like to shadow and send a message. Tell them not to be shy!

The message could say something like this: "I'm 13 years old (or whatever age applies). I'm interested in following a career path similar to yours. Would you allow me to spend part of a day with you, shadowing and learning more about what you do?"

Chances are, the first person they ask will say no or won't respond at all. Chances are, the first 20 might yield the same results. So what? Have them ask 25, or even more. We're talking about their future! Doesn't it make sense to be persistent? They're researching and assessing the kinds of jobs and careers that they may be interested in exploring further, and the information they gather will help them make a good decision about the rest of their lives.

What if they have absolutely no idea what they want to do? Taking a personality test might give some guidance. These assessments are often given by the career services department of a college or offered by a high school counselor. The test will ask many questions. The answers will help assess traits and interests and offer suggestions for career paths that may be suitable.

Maybe they've decided they want to follow their heart and pursue something they're passionate about. That's great! But can they make a living at it? If they can't, then it shouldn't be their career—it should be their hobby. Don't let them become discouraged; there are still many choices that can bring them close to their passion.

Let's consider a young, talented basketball player. Odds are slim that this youngster will become a professional player. Even so, teaching and/or coaching for a high school or college, working for an arena in operations management, becoming a scout or going into marketing for a professional team could be possible.

There is a book that can help—*What Color is Your Parachute?* by Richard Nelson Bolles. It's full of exercises that connect areas of interest to possible career paths. Here are some examples:

- **Interested in fashion and beauty:** They could be a costume designer for plays or movies. They could work on set design or become a hair stylist or make-up artist.

- **Find satisfaction when things are in order and enjoy working with numbers:** Maybe they'd like to work in finance as an accountant, auditor, or analyst. They could work for any type of business since all businesses need finance folks. Perhaps they'd enjoy being an operations manager in a company or a paralegal. Or maybe they'd thrive in work as an information technology specialist, or in sales, customer service, working for an insurance or brokerage company, or as a tax or business attorney.

- **Find joy in advocating for and helping others:** They could think about a career path in criminal justice, such as with the police force. Other options could include becoming a paralegal, lawyer, counselor, teacher, real-estate broker, or an operations manager. Nonprofits are great outlets to serve a community or to feed a passion. If they are gregarious and have good public-speaking skills, they might choose to be a trial lawyer. Introverts might choose to be a researcher, or a business or tax lawyer. A personal experience, like a difficult divorce in their own family, may lead them to become a family attorney.

- **Enjoy working outside or with their hands:** They could become a construction worker, electrician, plumber, floor installation specialist, heating and cooling specialist, project manager, auto or plane mechanic, pilot, chef, baker, food scientist, park ranger, bartender, or a building inspector.

- **Fulfilled by creativity:** They might like to be a writer, editor, proofreader, artist, graphic designer, or architect.

Even doctors have different personalities that suit the path they choose. Some practice general medicine, which requires them to see and talk with patients, while others choose to do the research.

See how talents and interests can be combined to fit into many different industries? Explore them with your teen and find those they enjoy. Look for what makes them happy and gives them energy. After all, wouldn't it be nice for them to make a living at something that didn't feel like work?

Explore all the options.

If your teen's school offers a career fair, have them attend it. These events introduce many kids to career options they never considered and can give them direction.

Let's step back to consider why some kids are exposed to events like this while others are not. Kids from some families aren't encouraged by the adults in their lives to check out these kinds of events. Kids, and maybe their parents, don't know anyone who has a bigger, better job. Their parents have jobs that don't thrill them—jobs that simply allow them to get by. Maybe these parents complain about their bosses, about their pay, about the hours they work, and the tasks they perform. This doesn't inspire kids to think positively about their own career path. It's a tragedy that these young people might consider work a necessary evil—something to be tolerated and dealt with rather than something to embrace.

It doesn't need to be like that. Work is the opportunity to earn, to produce, and to empower oneself financially. When a career path allows someone to use inherent talents, work also becomes an opportunity to make a positive difference. This is how parents should encourage their kids to think.

However, some parents—especially those who struggle to get by financially—just want their kids to have something secure and stable. They tell them to apply at one of the biggest companies in town, or with the government, because of the security and benefits they believe will come with such a job.

These might be the right choices for some. There's something to be said for security and benefits. But taking whatever job is available with Uncle Sam, or with The Very Large Corporation of America, isn't necessarily going to be a rewarding experience. And just because it offers a degree of stability doesn't mean it will provide an opportunity for high-level earnings.

The security of jobs like this can be overrated too. During difficult times, big corporations often announce mass layoffs, and they sometimes go through mergers after which not all positions remain intact.

Still, a stable, work-a-day job might be the right choice for some. If it is what your teen wants, then tell them to go get it. But parents serve their kids better when they help them find out what they'd really like to do.

Remember this: The real value of helping your children find good careers is that it will allow them to accumulate and deploy wealth, not just to pay the bills and barely get by. The psychology of money is scary for some people and empowering for others. Choosing careers they love will help kids excel and put them in the best possible position to attain the lives they want to live—now and in the future.

Figure it out first.

I remember when my daughter was trying to figure out what she wanted to do. She was interested in math and science and was considering becoming a physician's assistant. I encouraged her to visit with some—spend a half day with them. She did and, as a result, devised a serious career goal.

It's a good idea for young people to figure out the path they want to follow before enrolling in college. This way, their college experience leads to the career they really want.

Every potential career path is accompanied by questions to consider. Maybe your child loves cooking and thinks becoming a chef sounds like a good career path. But are they prepared to work every Friday and Saturday night—and holidays, too? That's when chefs are most in demand, after all.

Maybe your child is intrigued by real estate and likes the fact that it doesn't require a college education (although a business degree wouldn't hurt). They'd have flexibility in their work schedule, but do they really want to hold open houses every Saturday and Sunday afternoon and evening while the rest of the world is relaxing, watching sports, or out having fun?

Construction is challenging and interesting. Drywalling and tiling require real skill, and experts can be rewarded nicely for their work. But it's very hard, physical labor. Are they prepared for that?

Attorneys help people, and their billing rates are unbelievable. They also go through long stretches when they don't see their families. Will your child be willing to make that kind of sacrifice?

Being a doctor is often an aspiration. Is your child ready to commit to the time and expense it takes to become one? If they choose to be an OB-GYN or surgeon, are they willing to get up in the middle of the night to deliver babies or perform surgery?

It's important that your children ask themselves hard questions like these.

Remember my daughter and how she shadowed physician's assistants to see if that kind of work might be right for her? After a lot of consideration, she chose to go into commercial real estate instead. The nature of the work suited her better, even though it required her to live solely on income earned on commissions. This took some adjustments—especially since she only made one or two sales each year. But she got used to it and did quite well. Those few commissions were her entire income, but when she got a deal done, it was a big one. After seven years as an investment real-estate professional, she decided to follow in my footsteps and join my financial-planning and wealth-management company. She is currently working as the marketing and operations director. The experience she gained in her job as a real-estate professional was invaluable and, like many first careers, lead to a new venture when she was looking for a change.

Do they need college?

Many young people graduating from high school are under some pressure to go to college. That might or might not be the right choice. Is it the best path for the career they want? If that career is a doctor or an engineer, then yes, college is a must. If not, maybe there's another way without the time and expense of a four-year college degree. For many careers, college isn't required. Encourage them not to get stuck in the traditional pattern of thinking that every high school graduate must go to college. Training for many careers can be found outside of the traditional four-year-college route. Help them find their own path and follow it.

I have a client whose son absolutely hated school. He liked to be outdoors and wanted a career that would allow him to work outside. He started a lawn-mowing business and did well. It blossomed into a full-scale landscaping business. Now he has a crew and several trucks, and he's outside all day.

How well is he doing? He's doing well enough to offer his employees a pension and a 401(k), which our company manages for him.

He didn't go to college. He just pursued something he enjoyed. Of course, he had to learn a lot about running a business along the way—finance, marketing, personnel management, and many other things. But he learned all of it—and without a college degree.

Another client's son loved working out in the gym. His mom suggested that he might be a good physical therapist. They explored that path and realized how much schooling was involved. Since he didn't love school, they agreed that this wasn't the right choice for him. He loved building things, however. Even as a young child, he had always loved helping his dad with decks and other projects. He decided that he could combine his fitness level and his love of working with his hands to pursue a career in construction. Now he's happy and doing well in a profession that suits him.

Today's workforce is very agile. Internships and entry-level positions allow young adults to explore careers that interest them, before or instead of college. Let's say your child has always wanted to go into a career in graphic design. College is certainly one pathway for this, but so is an internship at a design agency. They could invest in software and take online courses while also working alongside seasoned design professionals. They'll have access to experts whom they can ask for tips and advice. They can start when they're 18 or 19 years old, and it won't cost tens of thousands of dollars a year like college would. After they decide that this is truly the career for them, they can still get the degree if needed.

I recently talked to a client who has an adult son who is very successful in the computer-technology industry. When he was in fifth grade, he convinced his parents to let him take their family computer apart because he thought it was too slow. They hesitated, and it took a lot of convincing, but they finally gave in. To their amazement, their son made the computer three times faster! In high school, he was known as the "computer whiz." While he was in college, a technology company offered him a job, and he dropped out to work full time. His parents were concerned…at first. He now earns more than both of his parents put together.

His parents held fast to the conventional wisdom that says kids won't get a good-paying job without a degree. There's some truth to it, in some cases. They'll probably get a better-paying first job with a degree. A college graduate could start at $50,000-plus a year in a junior position, while a high school graduate might start out in an entry level position making $15 an hour.

But the high school graduate is also four years younger and isn't saddled with $100,000 in student loan debt. And the high school graduate can learn directly in the work environment, whereas the college graduate had to take sociology and chemistry in order to earn enough credits for the degree.

The high school graduate's first job, even if it pays less than a college graduate can make, still provides the opportunity to develop skills and build experience.

That can be the first step on a path to advancement and career success. If a person does well enough in that first job, there's going to come a point in their career ascension when no one cares—or even asks—if they have a degree.

So, which is better? College or no college? That's not my point. I simply want you to see that there are many paths to follow to find a chosen career. Help your kids identify theirs and put together a plan to achieve it.

Don't listen to the naysayers.

Many adults have never really had a career-type job. They've always been in a punch-the-clock-and-stay-out-of-trouble type of job. It can be difficult for them to think in more ambitious terms. But I've never talked to a parent who didn't want their kids to do even better in life than they did. When you look at your kids, you shouldn't just see a younger version of yourself who will probably follow the same path. Instead, you should see a young person for whom the sky is the limit.

If they have the idea that they aren't cut out for a career, and that they should simply accept a low-wage, no-potential-for-advancement job, encourage them to get rid of it now. If they want that kind of work, that's fine, but only if it's a decision they make with a complete understanding of their options.

Don't let the cynics discourage them from pursuing their career dreams. Often, kids are told they can't do well because of their grades. They're told to accept less than what they want because they don't go to college. Or maybe they go to college, but not to an elite school. Or they're told they lack the traits necessary to pursue a lucrative career. These are someone else's opinions—and often, these naysayers were similarly influenced by someone else. Tell your kids not to listen to them.

Every young person, no matter the disadvantages they face, can aspire to do better. All they need is a good mentor, some wise direction, and the right opportunities to learn and grow.

Now ask them what it is they'd really like to do.

Got the answer? Good. Tell them not to stop until they've got a plan to accomplish it.

"If you're saving with the goal of college in mind, good. Keep it up!"

—Jill Gleba

CHAPTER 6

Solving the Mysteries of College Costs

This chapter is written especially for a parent or guardian who is helping a child with college and career decisions. But it might be for you, too. If you're thinking of changing careers or starting college later in life, many of the same principles apply. Your workplace may pay for college if it relates to your career. Additional training and education may help you advance in your career, get better pay, or simply find a job that fulfills you.

College is expensive. It's in the news a lot. People are paying attention to the debt from student loans that college graduates carry—an average of $37,173 per student and more than $1 trillion nationwide.

So, is college worth the cost? That's a fair question.

It's not uncommon for a four-year degree to cost $80,000 or more when you consider all the associated costs. If your child qualifies for a student loan, it's easy to tell yourself that the money they'll make with the degree will put them in a position to pay it back.

For some young people, however, college is not a wise investment of four years of time and tens of thousands of dollars. Instead, they can work their way into good-paying careers with grit and determination—by relentlessly pursuing opportunities and making the most of them—while never setting foot in a college classroom. College is not for everyone, and many people manage quite well without obtaining a degree.

If they do choose to go to college, they'd be wise to do their homework and learn about options available to ease the pain of the price tag. College is a good value for many people, but financially, it's a cost/benefit proposition. My goal is to help find the most economical way to do it. The more costs can be reduced, the more the proposition will work in favor of attending.

And, of course, as we said in the previous chapter, figuring out what they want to do after graduation can also save a lot of money. Changing courses midway means spending additional time and money on classes to fulfill the requirements. The additional education still has value; knowledge is always a positive step. But wouldn't it be better to put the time, effort, and money toward a career they really want, knowing that the outcome will help them build their future and can keep them motivated? It makes financial sense.

Ease the pain of the price tag.

In 2021, the average cost of a two-year college was about $10,000 per year. A four-year college averaged $26,600 per year. For graduate school, the cost was an average of $43,500 per year. And the prices are rising astronomically—at about double the rate of inflation!

How do you plan for an expense like this? If you plan to send your kids to college, I hope you've already started saving.

You can always count on your assets—assuming, of course, that you have assets. But there are many, many other places to find funding. And while there are no guarantees, most high school graduates have options to help defray expenses. It's important to understand what the options are and how they work.

We've already explored ways to save money—and how to make it work for you—in earlier chapters. I won't repeat it all here. If you're saving with the goal of college in mind, good. Keep it up!

How much do you need save? A lot. But if your child attends a community college for the first two years ($10,000 a year) before transferring to a four-year college to finish out a degree ($26,600 a year), you will save close to $33,000.

Maybe your child can take an accelerated program that can be completed in three years, instead of four. Maybe they can get ahead by earning college credits while still in high school. These, and a few extra college classes each semester, also make it feasible to finish in three years. How does this help? First, they'll knock off an entire year of room-and-board. Second, they can start earning money a whole year earlier. It's not an easy proposition, but it can be done.

Tap into the grandparents! Obviously, they can't all afford it. If they can, ask them. Here's an interesting fact: If a grandparent gives a grandchild a gift exceeding $16,000 (gift tax limit for 2022), the grandparent is required to report the gift to the IRS and file a gift tax return Form 709. However, if they pay their grandchild's college tuition directly to the school, it's not considered a gift and is tax-free.

A contribution to someone else's 529 college savings plan is also subject to the $16,000 gift exclusion rule. A special regulation in the tax code enables donors to use up five years' worth of exclusions and make a one-time gift of $80,000 to a 529 (in 2022) without requiring the child to pay taxes on the gift.

And, did you ever consider negotiating the cost of college? Colleges may tell you their rates are hard and fast, but don't be so sure. Many colleges will negotiate packages. They want enrollment and they may be willing to listen.

Other ways to pay for college include:

- **Bank loans.** You'd be wise to exhaust all other avenues first because you're going to take on a lot of debt and interest obligations if you go this route.
- **529 plans.** Parents can put assets into an account that remains tax-free as long as it's used to pay for college and college-related expenses.

- **Uniform Transfers to Minors Account (UTMA).** This is an investment account that belongs to the child but can be managed by an adult until the child is of age. When the child reaches the age of 18 or 21 (depending on state rules), the account becomes theirs.

- **State-based education trust.** This product allows parents to purchase years of college in advance, with payments or a lump sum while the child is still young.

- **Military service.** The military will sometimes commit to pay for college education as long as enough time is served.

- **An annuity.** Actually designed for retirement, this financial tool can be used to pay for college if the parent is 59-and-a-half years or older when the student enters college.

- **Life insurance policy.** You can add extra money to your policy that grows tax-free and can be used for college.

- **Gifting.** Funds are exempt from the usual gifting limits (and thus taxation) if used to pay for college.

Weigh the options.

I know a very smart high school student who was accepted into a top-tier school, but with no scholarship. He was also accepted into another school—good, but not top-tier—with a full scholarship. Choosing the second school would save nearly $100,000. But it's a tough choice. He'll need to consider whether the top-tier school attracts better recruiters, which could lead to the possibility of a better first job. And after the first job, would this even matter? Is the student planning to go on to post-graduate study? Will his choice affect his chance of being accepted into the next college? Is it worth the money?

Give your student the opportunity to explore campuses and get a feel for the schools' environments.

- Visit colleges and walk campuses.

- Meet with an admissions counselor and verify the admissions requirements.

- Determine all of the actual costs—not just the class expenses, but average book costs, room-and-board, and meal plans.

- Ask about financial-aid opportunities and work/study programs (which often fill up fast).

- Explore jobs available for your student in the area.

- Investigate the academic programs and see if the college has partnerships with any companies for possible internships.

- Ask if your student can attend a class before enrolling.

- Discuss the chances for success in admission, graduation, and placement into the job market. After all, the purpose of attending college is to get onto the right career path.

Talk to your child about the finances.

For many families, the cost of college is the elephant in the room. You'd love to shell out money for whatever school your child chooses, but it's a huge expense. My advice? Underpromise what you feel you can contribute. You may start off by saying something like, "We will have saved (X) by the time you start college, and after that, we should be able to contribute (Y) each year." This avoids misunderstandings and allows your child to build their own financial plan, with your contributions plugged in.

If your student is interested in two different schools that are far apart in cost, you might offer to fund the same amount for both colleges with the understanding that they will have to borrow the difference if they choose the higher-priced option.

There are helpful online calculators that break down what it costs to borrow money. For instance, if a student borrows $27,000 at 6.8 percent interest, their payment will be $311 each month. If the loan is $45,000 at 8.5 percent, they'll pay $558 each month to pay back the loan. The idea is to take a big, abstract loan amount and translate it into a month-to-month reality. Before they borrow money for their education, be sure they understand their obligation and the payment they'll be responsible for after graduation.

Determine how much he or she will need to borrow and show them an amortization table. This breaks down principal and interest payments that will be due each year. Your student will be able to see clearly what will be necessary to pay back the amount borrowed.

It's important for parents to help their kids avoid too much debt. Unlike most other types of debt, student-loan debt cannot generally be discharged in bankruptcy. In the case of default, the federal government can garnish wages or intercept tax refunds to recover the money.

If there's a silver lining, it's that many parents believe their kids get more out of college when they are at least partly responsible for its costs rather than receiving an open-ended blank check from the parents. Being on a financial hook, even a small one, may encourage students to live more frugally, choose courses more carefully, and hit the books with more commitment.

Many parents offer their kids more than they can afford to contribute, risking their own retirement. Don't do it. Let them borrow money and help them out later, if you can. The best gift you can give your kids is to be financially prepared for your own retirement, so you won't have to move in with them later!

Financial aid is available.

Few know all the ins and outs of financial aid. It can be mind-numbing, but the more you know, the better you'll be able to leverage dollars that help defray college costs. Stay with me, we'll walk through it.

Fill out the Free Application for Federal Student Aid (FAFSA).

The FAFSA is used by all high schools and can be applied to any college. It's available online or at high schools. It can be a bit intimidating for people not accustomed to paperwork, but there is plenty of help available online and, hopefully, through your child's high school.

There are questions on it about the parents' and the child's assets, and the expected costs of the college the child wants to attend. Retirement assets—such as 401(k) plans, IRAs, annuities, or other plans—do not need to be included. The child's assets are the primary consideration when determining eligibility for aid.

Depending on your answers, a calculation will be made based on one of two formulas. The first is based on federal and state methodologies. The second is based on the rules and priorities of the institution the child wants to attend.

Upon completion of the FAFSA, you and the school(s) your child is interested in attending will receive a Student Aid Report. The school(s) will consider the report, the expected family contribution, and the ability to borrow funds to determine eligibility for aid. There may be forms needed in addition to the FAFSA, and many schools will also want to see tax returns—so make sure they're up to date.

Eligibility for students under age 24 is, with some exceptions, based on their parents' income. Students older than 24 are considered independent of their parents, and eligibility is based solely on their own income and assets.

Learn about the different kinds of financial aid.

There are two basic kinds of financial aid for students. The first is need-based, which is determined by income and assets. The second is merit-based, which is based on factors like SAT scores, sports achievements, or other talents.

Financial aid can come in the form of grants, loans, or work-study arrangements. Most families who make under $100,000 a year can qualify for some type of financial aid.

If your student is considering a loan, make sure they understand the different types available. Some loans are subsidized. This means that the federal government will pay the interest while they are students. Others are unsubsidized which means the borrower is charged interest on the loan amount even while still a student. An unsubsidized loan accumulates interest while the student is going to school. If you have the option, accept a subsidized loan over an unsubsidized loan.

The Perkins Loan is a low-interest federal loan for those in greater need. These are funded with federal dollars and are disbursed through a school's financial-aid office.

Grants, unlike loans, do not have to be repaid. A Pell Grant, for instance, is a grant subsidized by the federal government and is awarded only to undergraduate students who display exceptional financial need and have not earned a bachelor's, graduate, or professional degree.

The Pell Grant program generally provides aid to low-income families who would otherwise not be able to afford the cost of higher education. There is no specific income limit for a Pell Grant, but it's necessary to first demonstrate financial need. This is calculated by taking the expected family contribution (EFC), subtracting the cost of attendance (COA) at the chosen school, and looking at the difference. To apply for a Pell Grant, you will need to fill out a FAFSA and qualify for financial aid.

When a student is particularly attractive to colleges, schools will sometimes get into a bidding war to entice them. In this case, it's often possible to negotiate financial aid packages.

Beware of scammers. There are companies that claim they will get you lots of money to put toward college. Be skeptical. If you are pressured into giving anyone a check, a checking account number, or a credit card to sign up for a service like this, walk away. If you are told that a program can adjust your income and/or assets to make it seem like you earn less money, thereby qualifying for more aid, don't go near it. Such practices are frequently illegal.

These defrauders are different from legitimate companies that have made it their business to assist students in getting into the college of their choice, however. These companies train students for college entrance tests for those who struggle with test taking, for example. High school guidance counselors can often recommend companies for this.

Here are some other claims to avoid:

- **"For a fee, we provide a comprehensive list of scholarships."** Do not spend money on a fee-based matching service. The biggest and best scholarship databases are available for free on the internet.

- **"Billions of dollars of award monies go unclaimed."** Statements about funds going unclaimed are simply untrue. If funds are available, students will compete for them.

- **"We have a money-back guarantee."** Legitimate scholarships are always competitive. No one can guarantee that you will win a scholarship.

- **"We need your credit card or bank account number."** No legitimate scholarship should require your credit card or bank account numbers.
- **"We will do all the work."** To receive a scholarship, students must complete the applications and essays themselves. No one else can do the work for them.

College isn't for everyone, and it's very expensive. It's in the best interests of both students and parents to know the options available. Take time to explore them and learn as much as you can. Pursue those that seem right for you and your scholar. I've provided more information about college saving and funding on my company website, GlebaAndAssociates.com. Your diligence now may be able to help you send your child to college without it becoming a financial hardship.

"Among the many things new entrepreneurs must learn, perhaps none is more important than how to find customers."

—*Jill Gleba*

CHAPTER 7

Thinking of Starting Your Own Business?

Two clients, both residents of Metro Detroit, worked at a boiler company. They never intended to be business owners; they just wanted to hang onto their jobs.

But the longer they worked there, the more they were bothered by the way the owner ran the business. Day in and day out, things would happen that prompted them to think, "We could do this better."

Could they?

One of them was good at taking calls and dealing with customers. He set up appointments, worked the books, and ran the operational side of things. The other made service calls and took care of customers' needs. Their strengths complemented each other, and they knew the industry.

Could they break out on their own? Could they make it work? Could they make money? Probably not on the day they opened their doors. Most companies don't.

Questions like these often present themselves to people who are thinking of starting a business. They envision themselves succeeding, but it's hard to navigate across the bridge from where they are to the place they visualize.

Don't quit your day job yet.

Maybe you're ready to set up shop. I hope you'll think about running your business part-time at first, while hanging on to your full-time job and bringing in an income as someone else's employee. You might not like this suggestion. I get that. After all, you'd be working two jobs at the same time, possibly for months on end. That would be hard on you and your family.

You'd rather just go at your own business full-bore. After all, customers expect you to be available during normal business hours. That's a hard expectation to meet when you're working for someone else full time.

It's psychologically tough, too. After all, once you've made the decision to move on, it's extremely difficult to show up at the office every day and stay engaged. It's hard to work as part of a team that's pursuing success for a company that you're not going to be part of for much longer.

I understand all these reasons to ditch your current job and put your heart and soul into your new venture. But there are good arguments for sticking it out. My job is to look out for the financial well-being of my clients; a situation in which people are working like crazy and earning no income does not fit with that. Even if you've saved up the recommended six months' worth of living expenses, you'll start depleting those resources the day you leave your job.

Maintaining your current salary while building a revenue base with your start-up adds to your savings while preparing a smooth exit from your current position.

In the meantime, do the prep work. There's a lot that can be done ahead of time and outside normal business hours. Assemble your marketing materials. If you'll need it, look for office space. Develop a customer base. Work on perfecting your products and services. Secure vendors and write proposals. You might need to make creative use of a lunch hour here and there. Starting a business isn't easy. If you can navigate these challenges, it's an indication that you can also run a business.

Leaving your job before your business generates the revenue needed to support yourself can cause a slew of problems. You might be forced to take on jobs that aren't in your best interest, or you might offer discounts just to get some money coming in. Pretty soon, you will be over-servicing a customer who's underpaying.

You could borrow money and take on debt, if you can get it. Banks are reluctant to lend money to startups with no capital and no track record. Even if you can, saddling yourself with a huge financial obligation right off the bat isn't the best way to establish your new company.

Some borrow money backed by the equity in their home. It's a quick and easy way to get money, but it's tricky. The equity in a home is strictly theoretical. Just because your home is appraised at a certain value doesn't mean it will sell for that amount. Yet, if that amount is borrowed, it will all have to paid back, plus interest.

It's easy to see why prospective entrepreneurs might believe they have no choice but to get that loan. After all, if they want to open a gym, they need equipment. If they want to open a factory, they need machinery. Capital is essential when you're starting a business, and it's understandable that many would-be entrepreneurs have a hard time seeing where it will come from.

Ramping up gradually makes more sense, especially if you can save during this period. If you save at least part of the capital you'll need, you'll be in better financial condition. This is important as you prepare to open your doors. It's hard enough to make the money needed to cover normal business expenses. If you add loan payments to this, you'll squeeze your profit margins even tighter.

If you're married, you might rely on the full-time paycheck of a spouse while you get the ball rolling. Not everyone has this option, of course, and that income would have to be enough to cover all your personal expenses. If this works for you, great! You have the freedom to pour yourself into your new venture without undue pressure.

Know your business.

This seems obvious, but an important element of a business startup is to have some experience working in the industry in which you'll operate.

The restaurant industry is brimming with people who dream of owning a restaurant. They open their doors based solely on their dream. Many have never worked a day of their lives in a restaurant. They've eaten in plenty of them, and they've watched many episodes of *Restaurant: Impossible* on Food Network, so they're convinced they can make it work.

Small, independent retail stores also tend to attract starry-eyed entrepreneurs. It's not that they lack talent or work ethic. It's that learning all the ins and outs of an industry while working on the job as an owner is very risky.

The clients who started the business selling boilers knew the industry—they'd worked in it! They knew what customers were looking for. They understood what made a quality product. They were aware of the resources and suppliers they needed. Their knowledge made it plausible for them to hit the ground running right from the start.

Do you want to own a restaurant? Spend a year or two working in some first. Learn about their operations. Pay attention to everything—from purchasing to server schedules to what kind of equipment the dishwashers need. It's worth the investment of your time to be certain you know what you're doing. Then, once you get your business going, you can enjoy a lifetime of success.

No customers, no business.

Among the many things new entrepreneurs must learn, perhaps none is more important than how to find customers.

Quality is essential. Good management is crucial. Sound financial management is absolutely necessary. You can be good at all those things, but if you don't know how to find customers, none of them matter.

This trips up many entrepreneurs. Maybe the company they came from had an effective sales team. Their role, however, was in the production department. They know sourcing, but what about sales work? That doesn't always come naturally. Many people feel about as awkward in sales as they would putting a suit on backward.

But there's no getting out of the sales piece. If you sell professional services, you'll need to reach out to companies to find those interested in becoming clients. If you open a restaurant, you need to get people in the door. If you sell industrial products, you need to let companies know what you have to offer.

Think you could just hire a sales manager? It's possible, but that could be a risky investment in the early stages of your company's life. The ultimate responsibility for finding customers is yours.

There are resources that can help. There are excellent how-to books on sales. You can find many videos on YouTube. You can make connections and gain insight from professionals through local business organizations. The biggest mistake you can make is to do nothing. If you feel uncomfortable with sales, you will have to learn to deal with being uncomfortable. The success of your business depends on it.

What's it all *really* going to cost?

You need to understand the real costs of running a business from the start. This is important to get right. Many new business owners low-ball their costs and end up with an unpleasant surprise when they see what they're really spending.

Let's pretend you're a massage professional. You rent office space for $2,500 a month. Then, you buy a professional massage table for between $600 and $1,000. You purchase the supporting material such as creams, oils, lotions and so forth, costing several hundred dollars each month.

Initially, the overhead doesn't seem too bad—but you're not done. You'll also need a marketing budget—maybe $500 to $1,000 a month—so you can let people know you're in business. You'll need to spend some of your professional time doing the marketing work yourself since you can't afford to hire someone else yet.

You may need to purchase custom scheduling software. Outlook or Google Calendars might work, but you need to be sure the system you choose is right for you.

Oh, and you'll want to pay yourself. I don't think $50,000 a year is unreasonable for a startup business owner, but you'll have to consider for yourself the amount you'll need to earn to make it work.

In this scenario, how much will your business need to earn to break even? It would take at least $8,000 a month. Of course, breaking even isn't the goal. You want to be profitable. But let's first assess what it would take to break even, then we'll go from there.

Let's say your company charges $75 for an hour-long massage. You'd need to do 107 massages a month to break even. If you work six days a week—and I'm assuming you're willing to work Saturdays to meet the demands of your customers—you'd have to do an average of five massages each day to meet the threshold.

Keep in mind that an eight-hour day, including a lunch break and the time needed between appointments to clean up and reset, allows for six or seven time slots. So, probably the most you can do is seven massages a day. Let's say you average six. You'd pull in a little less than $11,000 per month. Your profit margin would be about $3,000 a month, assuming you control the costs beyond the overhead we've already identified.

This might sound good. But are you sure you can attract enough business to fill all those slots? Do you have time to do all the necessary marketing and still do that many massages?

Only once the business is consistently doing better than break-even can you consider the next steps to building a successful venture like plans for future growth, hiring, or expanding your facilities. When should you add more tables? What about the cost of transforming your space into a spa-like atmosphere?

There are alternatives to jumping in with both feet. Maybe, instead of opening a storefront right away, you could rent a massage chair from another business, keep your full-time job, and give massages during the off-hours. This limits risk and gives you the opportunity to build a loyal clientele. Once you've worked this angle for a while, you might be in a better position to make the financial commitments of a full-time business.

Prospective business owners should always think through details like this. Go through a thorough analysis first. Don't get your heart set on doing things a certain way and in a certain time frame. Be willing to adjust your plans to stay on a healthy long-term path to success. Your goal isn't to just meet expenses. It's to create wealth—both for today and for your future.

Plan for your future.

When entrepreneurs start, they often work tirelessly just to stay afloat. That's understandable. It takes time to learn how to run a business, build a customer base, and acquire the resources needed. I admire those willing to make the sacrifice.

But sacrifice isn't a long-term outlook. Your goal should be to get into a position to reward yourself for hard work. You'll collect a paycheck, but that's only the start. You should also reward yourself by setting money aside for your retirement. This is hard for a lot of entrepreneurs to wrap their heads around, especially in the first few years, when they feel they need to pour everything into the business. At some point, however, they should ask themselves why they started the business and who they're doing it for.

I recently worked with a client who started a business with three partners. They had no other employees. They weren't putting money aside. The business was new, but they needed to start planning for their own futures now—even if putting away only a small amount was all that was possible. It would have been even better had they started from day one, but we discussed some options to start now.

I explained that they could put money in IRAs, one for each partner. We also considered a Simplified Employee Pension (SEP) plan. This plan allows a business to save money for retirement while subtracting the amount from the taxable revenue. Since these employers were also the employees, this was a good option for them. They just needed to decide what percentage of their income they could comfortably set aside.

Plan for your employees' futures, too.

Many business owners did not intend to own a business, but an opportunity arose, and they jumped at it. They have experience, product knowledge, and know how to attract and serve customers. Some companies stay small and profitable. Others grow—suddenly there's a need for ten more employees. When this happens, owners will need to slowly hire help so they can stay focused on their vision. They'll want to train employees to help run the day-to-day activities of the business—passing along the tasks that other professionals specialize in like payroll, human resources, and information technology. Many of these things can be fielded on a part-time basis.

Attracting and keeping good employees may seem overwhelming. But you will find that employees stay when they are rewarded and treated with respect. A retirement plan is a nice benefit to offer.

If you're a single employer/employee, look into a SEP plan. If you have employees to consider, you might choose a SIMPLE plan for yourself and your employees. It's similar to a 401(k) plan but with a lower contribution limit. The company matches employees' deposits dollar-for-dollar, up to a maximum of 3 percent of the employee's income. For instance, if the employee is earning $60,000 a year, the company would match their deposit up to $1,800 annually.

Matching a figure like 3 percent is usually not overwhelming for business owners. Yet, 3 percent can make a huge difference to an employee, setting them on the road to a healthier financial future. What if the employee in question also happens to be the owner? Well, then it makes perfect sense!

I believe it is a business owner's responsibility to help employees save for retirement. I am not advocating for anything that I don't do for my own employees. For most full-time employees, the income they receive from their employer is their only source. As a business owner, if you don't take an interest in helping them save for retirement, you make it much more difficult for them to plan for themselves. After all, what they need for that savings comes directly from you.

This is a big step for the employer, so take some time to consider the many types of retirement plans available to employers. Some are almost free, with the employees contributing without a match from the employer. Others are more expensive for the employer. Professionals who specialize in this field can guide you.

It's not easy.

One of the hardest things about owning a business is the effort required day after day—even when others think being the captain of your own ship means you can work when you want.

Business ownership may seem to some like a cushy gig, but owners can put in 60, 70, maybe 80 hours a week. They don't get overtime pay, and they won't get a promotion because they're already at the top. They could have kept their regular job, positioned themselves for raises, participated in the company's 401(k) program, took bonuses, and did their best to climb the corporate ladder. But instead, they prepared themselves for the ups and downs of business ownership and followed their dream.

So why do it?

Is starting a business difficult? It sure is. Does it involve risk? Definitely. But you work hard anyway. Why not work hard at something that is yours? Building a business could be the most powerful way for you to build wealth—not to mention a legacy for your life.

It's not for everyone, so think about it long and hard. Confront tough questions before you take the risk. If you're ready for the challenge, then go for it. Build your successful business. Your potential to generate wealth is theoretically unlimited. Don't accept any other vision for your company's success. Take care of yourself and take care of your employees—successful businesses do both. Expect and strive for the highest rewards possible. Set yourself up for retirement. Set yourself up to be generous. Envision wealth as your reward for your vision and hard work. If you can picture these things, then take the leap!

Don't go it alone.

There are a lot of resources available to help business owners. Some are free; others require an investment. Make the investment if the circumstances are right.

Chambers of commerce and other business organizations sometimes offer mentors to work with new owners. They also offer business roundtables and peer-to-peer groups to gain insight from others who have been in your shoes.

If you find a mentor willing to help you, find out how much time and attention they have available. I've seen the founders of businesses approach experienced CEOs and ask them to serve on their advisory boards. I've also seen experienced CEOs agree to do it. You'll never know if you don't try. You'll get the same results by not asking as you would by asking and being told no. Give it a shot.

If you have money available to invest, hire a business coach. I went this route, and I'm glad I did. My coach helped me accomplish a great deal. A coach can help you, too.

- They offer ideas for ways to uncomplicate your life and work experiences.
- They help develop a plan to accomplish your goals.
- They provide a systematic structure that can help you regroup and stay on track.

If you're starting a business, you probably have specific issues with which you'd like help. Find a coach who is strong in those areas. Appreciate that they will challenge you. They'll help you identify goals and steps to take in the pursuit of those goals. They'll hold you accountable to deadlines and tasks.

Not everyone likes the idea of submitting to accountability. But if you're serious, you'll get over your resistance quickly and embrace things that can help you become more successful, including someone who will occasionally push you.

Coaches and mentors can help you develop skills and build knowledge. They may help you recognize that you can't grow if you're the company's only producer. They can offer advice about hiring and managing employees.

Before long, you'll learn what it means to sit in the leadership chair—to give clear direction, to delegate, and to trust people to do the work you used to do by yourself.

CHAPTER 8

Retirement:
Plan It and Make It Happen

I was talking with an acquaintance at a party recently. He said he was ready to retire. He'd put in 30 years and felt like he was done working.

I understand that mindset. He was psychologically ready to move on to the next phase of his life—one that didn't involve waking up to an alarm clock and trudging off to work each day.

"Will you have enough income to retire?" I asked him.

He looked at me as if I were speaking another language. He hadn't thought about it in those terms. He was mentally ready for retirement. But financially, he was not ready.

He hadn't spent years saving and building up the sources of income that would replace his earnings, and sadly, he's not alone. Many people make the same mistake. They figure retirement is a rite of passage, something everyone will be able to do at some point. One way or another, they'll have what they need to live on.

It doesn't work that way. A comfortable retirement requires planning—and the earlier you start, the better. It involves learning to save, invest, and build wealth. I absolutely cannot overstate the importance of this.

When my firm works with a client, we first look at their total assets and assess the income these assets can provide. However, if the client hasn't looked ahead, there won't be many assets.

It's vexing for most people. They've spent their entire lives working so they could earn enough to cover living expenses. Now they're staring at the prospect of spending the rest of their lives not working, and still having to cover those same living expenses—without having any idea how many years that might be.

How is it even possible?

Had they started saving and investing early in life, it would have been possible. A comfortable retirement would have been possible if they'd built up the kinds of assets that allowed them to recreate the income they'd earned during their working years.

How do you recreate your income?

Generally speaking, a viable retirement income is built from a combination of four things:

1. Investments you can turn into income.

2. Social Security.

3. Pensions.

4. Part-time work.

These are the four items that will provide income during your retirement. Some might include expected inheritances as a fifth item. I don't recommend this because it's unpredictable. Let's consider someone who's 60-something and wants to retire soon. They have parents who are in their 80s or 90s. They figure their parents will leave an estate at some point, and that can be part of their plan. But there's no telling how long the parents will live. I've seen it happen too often that by the time the parents pass away, there really isn't much left to inherit. It's simply not something to count on.

If you've saved and invested wisely throughout the course of your life, however, you can count on the four items listed.

How much will you need to save?

So how much will you need for a comfortable retirement? A lot. Look at how much you're spending each month now and realize that you will still need this much during your retirement years. Most people don't consider this—or how they'll recreate that income when they retire.

Think about it this way. A good rule of thumb is that $1 million in savings will generate 3.5 percent each year of income. That's $35,000 a year. Maybe you can live on that. But for many, it can be jarring to realize that even by saving $1 million, investments will only bring in $35,000 a year before they start seriously depleting principal.

Can you live on $35,000 a year? It depends on your spending, so scrutinize it now. Go back several months and don't leave out anything. For instance, include expenses that are only paid every other month or quarterly.

Now consider the lifestyle you want to live once you're retired. Maybe you want to continue to spend money as you always have. But maybe you want to travel more or take part in activities in your community. Maybe you want to get your first dog. What will these things cost?

Then consider some weightier issues. Will you need to care for aging parents? What about special-needs children or other family members? Are your kids doing well on their own? Does it make sense for you to move to a smaller home? Are there purchases you need to make to facilitate your retirement lifestyle? What adjustments are you open to making? These are crucial questions because you can only succeed in retirement if you have a realistic sense of your expenses.

For couples, there's another heavy issue to consider. They need to be prepared for the time when one or the other passes. How much income will they have if the other goes first? Make a list of the assets, pensions, Social

Security, and any other income you'll receive. Then create three columns. In the first, list the income of both spouses. In the second, list the income of one spouse if they were alone. In the third, list the income of the other spouse if they were alone. Do each of these scenarios include the money necessary to cover expenses?

Let's add one more column for life insurance. Often, couples reaching their 50s consider canceling their policies. Their kids are grown, or they don't have kids at all. Their home will soon be paid off. Why keep paying for life insurance? Before you decide to ditch it, let me explain why you should consider holding on to it.

Imagine a retired couple, both collecting Social Security. When one dies, the other will lose one of the monthly Social Security checks they're accustomed to receiving. The money from the life insurance policy could be the way to replace it. For instance, a $250,000 policy could provide a $730-per-month income at a 3.5% withdrawal rate.

Maybe you're thinking that your house will be paid off by retirement age, and that will give you enough income to cover the difference. It's possible. But, unfortunately, in the later years, house payments are often replaced by medical bills.

It's a lot to think about. The bottom line is that, when you retire, you can change how much you spend, where you live, and how you live. What you can't change is how much you've managed to save. Those decisions were made throughout the course of your adult life. When retirement comes along, your income will be determined by how much you've accumulated during those years.

How Social Security works.

Everyone pays into Social Security throughout the course of their working life, and everyone can draw funds from it at an age established by federal law. How much you draw depends on how much you've paid into the system during your working years.

When can you start collecting? Let's explore options.

You can begin drawing Social Security as early as age 62. Or you can wait until full-retirement age, at around age 66. There is some debate over which option is better. The longer you wait, the higher your monthly payment will be. So, why wouldn't you want to wait to collect the higher amount?

Consider two people who are the same age. One will start receiving Social Security at age 62. The other will wait until age 66. The 62-year-old will receive $2,000 per month right away. The other will receive nothing until four years later, at which point the payment will be $2,500 per month.

The 62-year-old will collect $24,000 per year before the second person collects a penny. That's $96,000 during that four-year period. Once the second person starts collecting, the payment will be $500 more each month. But was it worth the wait? I'm not so sure.

It will take between 14 and 17 years to make up the difference. The second person will be in his 80s before catching up to the first person. If you're confident you're going to live into your 90s, there may be an advantage to having an extra $500 a month for all those years. But what are the chances? We'd all like to believe we'll live a healthy life well into our 90s, but you may not. And, if you only live to be 80, you'd be much better off if you'd started collecting at age 62.

Here's an exception. Let's say you've saved enough to live off the income from your investments for those first four years. In this case, you could justify taking the larger Social Security distributions when you turn 66. Or, if you started drawing your money at age 62, you could invest the money and probably earn enough on the returns to equal the payments you would have received had you waited until you were 66 to collect—if not more.

Maybe you're thinking you'll just keep your full-time job for a while and start collecting your Social Security at age 62. It doesn't work that way. Even though you can legally start taking Social Security at age 62, the federal government would rather you waited until you were older unless you absolutely need it. For this reason, those who start collecting at 62 are only allowed to earn around $19,000 per year (2022) via any kind of work. If you wait until your full retirement age (or later) to start taking benefits, you can work (and earn) as much as you want while still receiving your full benefits.

Your full retirement age is determined by the year you were born. Although it's subject to change, you can find yours on the following chart:

BIRTH YEAR	FULL RETIREMENT AGE
1943-1954	66
1955	66 and 2 months
1956	66 and 4 months
1957	66 and 6 months
1958	66 and 8 months
1959	66 and 10 months
1960 or later	67

For each year you wait between age 62 and full-retirement age, your expected monthly check increases about 5 percent. If you wait beyond full-retirement age, your monthly benefits go up about 8 percent for each year.

So, if you're still working full-time and earning a healthy paycheck, it might make sense to hold off and wait for the higher amount. The amount you'll be allowed to earn won't be limited, and your benefits will increase monthly for every year you wait.

You might also consider waiting if you're healthy and your family's history is one of serial longevity. If genetics suggest that you may live well into your 90s, the extra income could be helpful.

A rule that applies to married couples is something else to think about. Since the amount of their monthly payments is dependent on the amount each of them earned during their working lives, each of their benefits will be a different amount. When one of them passes away, the lower payment is the one that is dropped, and the surviving spouse will continue to collect the higher of the two payments.

They can use this as a strategy when planning for retirement. Let's say one spouse retires early. If the other continues working until full-retirement age, they'll be entitled to the higher benefit amount. When either spouse dies, the other is guaranteed to continue receiving that higher income. And you might be surprised to know that if you were married to someone for 10 years—even if you divorced—you would still have spousal rights to an ex's Social Security benefits.

Investments, taxes, and Medicare—oh my!

Your own personal savings can, and should, play a large role in your retirement plan. Let's look at some strategies that can make your money work for you now to give you the assets you need for a comfortable future.

There are two types of Individual Retirement Accounts (IRAs)—a traditional IRA and a Roth IRA. It's important to know the difference.

Money put into a traditional IRA is deposited pre-tax. Taxes are only paid on this income when you pull it out. Until then, the income is sheltered from taxation.

With a Roth IRA, taxes are paid before the money is added to the account. When you pull it out at retirement time, there are no taxes due—not even on the gains. This can be a real advantage.

With a traditional IRA, if you pull out enough money for a $6,000 purchase, you might need to deplete your account by $8,000 because you will need to pay taxes on the withdrawal. With a Roth IRA, if you need $6,000, you pull out $6,000 because you've paid taxes on that money before it went into the account.

The government doesn't want to wait forever for its tax money from your traditional IRA, however. They want their cut, and they'll eventually require you to start taking income from it—whether you want to or not (currently, this happens at age 70 or 72, but the age is subject to change).

If you were a great saver and you have considerable assets in your traditional IRA, you may consider waiting to collect Social Security and use your traditional IRA funds first. IRA funds will grow, and in many cases, require you to take a larger income than you need in your later years, which creates a lofty tax bill. This is worth mentioning although it is a great "problem" to have.

You can also control your IRA income—and the amount owed in income taxes during retirement—by converting some of the money in your traditional IRA to a Roth IRA. A Roth IRA does not require distributions, and withdrawals from it aren't taxed. Have a conversation about these things with your accountant and financial advisor. I'll remind you, these professionals are there for everyone—not just for the rich. Don't be hesitant to find someone you trust and with whom you are comfortable discussing these things.

There's also the Medicare piece of the retirement pie to consider. Medicare premiums are based on income. When you turn 65, the government starts pulling the premium directly out of your Social Security check. It's cheaper than just about any alternative on the private insurance market—usually a few hundred dollars a month cheaper—but the price of it goes up or down depending on income.

Withdrawals made from your traditional IRA for big purchases mean higher income, and thus, higher Medicare premiums. Let's say, for instance, that you have a sizable investment portfolio with hundreds of thousands of dollars in it. Let's also say you own a house on which you still owe $40,000. You might think it makes sense to pull $40,000 from your investment portfolio to pay off your house, thus saving yourself the cost of your mortgage payments.

It might make sense. But the government will consider that $40,000 part of your income and raise your Medicare premium accordingly. You need to weigh the savings from your mortgage payoff, versus the increased premium. Making major purchases like home improvements, cars, or vacations before you retire, will help you avoid being bumped into the next income bracket during retirement and hiking up your Medicare premium. Pulling funds from a Roth IRA won't show up as income on taxes and it won't affect your Medicare premiums. Do you see how important it is to understand all the implications of your assets? Here's a quick overview:

- **Traditional IRAs:** taxed as income when funds are pulled out; affects Medicare premiums.
- **Roth IRAs:** taxed pre-deposit; not taxed when withdrawn; will not affect Medicare premiums.
- **Annuities:** only the gains are taxed; gains will affect Medicare premiums.
- **Pensions:** taxed based on total income; affects Medicare premiums.
- **Social Security:** taxed based on total income; affects Medicare premiums.

Taxed, taxed, and taxed again.

At least half of the people who walk into my office don't understand how income taxes work. They believe that if they are in the 22% tax bracket, they pay 22% of their income in taxes. This isn't the case. Income taxes are figured on a graduated basis. Here is an example of the 2022 tax rates for a married couple filing jointly:

2022 TAX RATES FOR A MARRIED COUPLE FILING JOINTLY	
ANNUAL EARNINGS	TAX RATE
Between $0 and $20,550	10%
Between $20,551 and $83,550	12%
Between $83,551 and $178,150	22%
Between $178,151 and $340,100	24%
Between $340,101 and $431,900	32%
Between $431,901 and $647,850	35%
$647,851 and above	37%

As a married couple, if you earned a total of $100,000 for the year, your first $20,550 is taxed at 10%, the next part of your income up to $83,550 is taxed at 12%, and the last $16,450 of your income will be taxed at 22%. Your total tax ends up being 13.23% of your income. This is only an example, tax rates are subject to change.

Why is this important? Well, if you decide you want to pull out a large sum of money from your investments for a home improvement project or car, you may want to consider how this could affect your taxes. It could send you into the next tax bracket and cost quite a bit in taxes. A tax expert will have some helpful strategies. For instance, if you need $20,000 for a project, they may suggest taking $10,000 in one year, and another $10,000 in the next year if you are in the last quarter of a tax year. Or you may want to withdraw money from a taxable account and harvest the losses and gains to reduce your tax bill.

Take a look at all of your accounts with a tax professional and learn how they are taxed. Some accounts are tax-deferred—only the gains are taxed. Some are tax-free and are never taxed when you withdraw from them. Understanding this before you make a major withdrawal can save you a bundle.

There are many types of retirement income.

When someone retires, they often have a lump sum of money to invest that will produce income for their retirement. Usually, it comes from a pension lump sum or a 401(k). So, what do they do with it? I recommend three general choices to my clients: guaranteed income, non-guaranteed investments, or a hybrid (a combination of both). There are thousands of products that fall into each category, but don't be overwhelmed. I'll explain each category here, and a financial planner can help you choose how and where to invest. It's a big decision because the earnings from these investments will allow you to receive a monthly check and determine the amount you'll have to live on during your retirement years.

Are you looking for fixed or guaranteed income?

When I talk to clients about products and investments, I find that many of them want guarantees. They want a dependable monthly income, one that won't fluctuate with the market's ups and downs. A fixed-income product can do this for them. It's like "buying a pension." In exchange for a lump sum, they're promised a guaranteed income throughout retirement.

If they are married, the income will be there until both spouses pass. There's a "refund" feature so that their heirs get the remaining amount if they both die before depleting their original investment.

Sure, it's a product that provides a guaranteed income, and there is some comfort in that. But there is no flexibility with it. Once you buy it, it's yours. There is clearly more growth potential with an investment product, but if a guaranteed income is important, this may be the right choice.

Understand what you are buying. One of the most appalling situations I've seen was when an advisor sold an income-generating product designed for single people to a married couple. The couple needed the income to continue when one spouse died, but the product didn't work that way—it was designed for single people. The surviving spouse found herself with no income when her husband passed. That mistake could have been avoided if the advisor was competent.

What about investments?

Investments are flexible and have growth potential, but they aren't guaranteed. And when retirement comes, they'll need to provide you with income for the rest of your life. How does this work? Well, if your investments are earning 8% each year and you're withdrawing 3.5 percent annually (the amount my firm recommends), then your investments will continue to grow, and you'll have a steady, reliable income that hopefully keeps up with inflation.

Building a portfolio for retirement may be different than when you were accumulating money during your working years. Investments should match your goal, and for retirement, that means choosing a balanced or growth and income portfolio.

For those who have extra assets that are not needed for income, then this extra can be invested in a more aggressive growth portfolio. Growth portfolios are used to grow assets, and usually do not provide as many dividends or income.

Compare it to choosing a car. When you go to a dealership, you'll tell the salesperson how the vehicle will be used so they can help you find something appropriate. A two-seater sports car isn't suitable for a family with kids. Of course, if you have the means, and you have a family vehicle, then you may choose to buy that "extra" sports car to enjoy. You want to buy what's right for your situation.

The same logic goes into building a portfolio. If you are putting together a portfolio for retirement, it's wise to choose investments that provide growth and income. If you don't need income, choose a growth portfolio. If you don't have an emergency fund, invest conservatively. Different goals require different portfolios and when your goals change, so will your investments.

Many people are unnerved by the market's volatility. If this sounds like you, don't let it stop you—just invest more conservatively. Your portfolio won't grow as quickly, so you'll need to withdraw a smaller percentage so your investments will still earn more than you are withdrawing and keep you from running out of money.

It's a lot to think about. Financial planning is my profession, so I'm biased, but trust me, you'll do yourself a favor by enlisting the help of a professional.

Hybrid products: the best of both worlds.

Hybrid products offer the option of both a guaranteed income and the growth of investments. There are usually two parts: 1) an investment portfolio and 2) a rider that will provide a guaranteed income. This is a choice for someone who doesn't want to be "stuck" with a fixed-income product with no flexibility, but because they lack experience or can't stomach the market ups and downs, they're uncomfortable investing in a non-guaranteed investment portfolio. With a hybrid product they can have both.

There are many variations of hybrid products. We'll consider one example: Let's say you invested $100,000 in this hybrid product. First, you would choose investments for your portfolio. Congratulations, you're invested in the market. Now, for a cost, you can add a rider that will give you the security of knowing that if the market goes down, or if your investment goes to zero, you will still have a guaranteed income for life based on your original investment of $100,000.

Most people buy a product like this 5–10 years before they retire with the hope that their money will grow, thus increasing their income at retirement. They don't stress as much over the market volatility since they have a bottom-line guarantee. I remind clients who are considering this option, however, that the income is guaranteed, not your investment performance. There are many versions of hybrids, so talk to a professional who can show you several options before choosing the one for you. Understand what you're buying before you buy it.

What is a 401(k)?

A comedian once joked that she thought a 401(k) was a race! In a way, it is. It's a marathon run throughout your adult life that prepares you for a comfortable future when you retire.

Usually, a traditional 401(k) plan is offered by an employer, and employees contribute to it throughout their working years. It's essential. And it's the reason many people are able to retire comfortably.

Taxes greatly influence the planning of our financial futures, which is one of the reasons 401(k) accounts are so widespread. The money you contribute to a 401(k) is not taxed until you withdraw it at retirement. If you earn $60,000 and you contribute $10,000 pre-tax to a 401(k), you are only taxed on $50,000 for that year. And sometimes, an employer will match or contribute additional money to your 401(k). This additional contribution is also not taxed until it's withdrawn—a very nice benefit!

So, the tax benefits of a traditional 401(k) are:

- You are not taxed on your contributions to the 401(k), thus reducing your income taxes.
- You are not taxed on the growth while the account is growing over the years.
- You will only be taxed when you withdraw the money at retirement.

You can save a lot of money with a 401(k). In 2022, annual contributions to a 401(k) could be as much as $20,500. Those over 50 years of age could contribute as much as $27,000. And the limits go up every year. So, even if you're starting a little later in life, a healthy contribution like this will help you fund your retirement.

Choosing between a traditional 401(k) or Roth 401(k).

Contributions to the traditional 401(k) described above benefit you immediately by allowing you to defer paying taxes on the money until it is withdrawn in retirement. Then, you can make withdrawals as needed, but it isn't typically set up to provide a regular income. You won't get a monthly payment from it or have your taxes automatically withdrawn.

A Roth 401(k) is another option and different from a traditional 401(k) because you'll pay taxes before you make your contribution. The benefit? You don't owe any taxes on the money or its growth when it's withdrawn.

Though there are similarities, there is a big difference between a Roth 401(k) and a Roth IRA. If you earn more than a certain income, you are not allowed to buy a personal Roth IRA (there are income limits). However, there are no income limits when contributing to a Roth 401(k). This difference could be valuable for you.

Here's an example of how it might work. Let's say you need $20,000 for a car after you retire. If you withdraw the money from a traditional 401(k), you will also owe taxes on that withdrawal, so you will need about $24,000 to cover the money for the car and the taxes due. If you withdraw the funds from a Roth account, you will only need to withdraw $20,000 since there will be no taxes due.

You can pay your taxes now, or later. I like both and, if possible, suggest contributing to each.

What happens to your 401(k) when you leave your job?

People changing jobs may need to decide whether to keep their 401(k) account where it is or roll it into another type of account. They should compare the costs of the investments and understand what they want from the asset, including if they want their asset to provide a regular income upon retirement.

They'll also want to consider who controls the plan. If the assets are with a company 401(k), the plan is most likely the company's, not theirs. They are the participant, but the company picks the product and chooses the investments. And the company is likely charging fees. If you want to see what the internal fees are for a 401(k), you'll need to obtain a 408(b).

I had a client who did not want to roll over the money from her 401(k). Instead, she chose to "just leave it there." During the time it was there, the company was restructured and her 401(k) was frozen for several months. When she was ready to move the assets, she couldn't. She had to wait until the restructure was complete before regaining access to her account. It's fortunate that she wasn't retired and in need of income right away.

Another client was not as fortunate. She was retired, needed the money in her 401(k), but didn't have access. She was forced to charge her expenses on a credit card and borrow from her family until the situation was resolved.

These are risks you take when leaving your 401(k) with a company whose moves you can't control. It's yet another reminder that you want to be sure you have an adequate emergency fund—one that is not tied up in a retirement plan. Ideally during retirement, you'd have an emergency fund to cover expenses for up to 12 months—but a minimum of six months. The more extra money you set aside, the more flexibility you will have during retirement.

Remember, retirement can last a long time. Even if you have multiple assets that can serve as income sources, you don't want to use all of them for that purpose. You want to make sure you have plenty of money that will last for the long term. And hopefully, you will be around to need it!

The 401(k) is one of the most popular retirement savings methods, and you should start building it up as early in your career as you can. Not every employer offers a 401(k), so those who do should be considered premium employers as you consider where you want to work. Don't underestimate the value of an employer who cares about preparing you for your future.

Many of our clients have built considerable wealth by contributing to their 401(k). Do not pass up this opportunity!

What about pensions?

Pensions are less common today and are usually only offered by large corporations and government employers. They generally operate using formulas that consider years of service, age, and average salary to determine their worth.

In many cases, it's necessary to wait for a predetermined number of years before a pension is vested. It's only available to the employee after this period. If they retire too early, they will usually have to take cuts or discounts.

Pensions used to be of the "defined benefit" variety. Managers of the pension would invest money and hope for growth in the value of those investments. No matter how the investments did, however, the employee would get a predetermined amount as their benefit.

It's now more common to be offered a "defined contribution" pension in which employees put a certain amount into a 401(k) plan with an employer match. The benefit amount is based on how well the investment does. This protects the employer from covering massive losses if the investments don't do well. It also makes it harder to plan for retirement because the benefit isn't predictable.

All pensions are heavily regulated. If they do not pass their annual audit, the employer must put more funds into the plan so they can pass the funding tests. A 401(k) is also in a trust so the employer cannot touch their employees' accounts. Pensions are generally given by the employer, whereas the 401(k) is a plan for the employee to save money, and sometimes the employer matches or has a profit-sharing with a 401(k).

If you have a pension and you're getting ready to retire, a financial advisor can help you figure out how to draw from it and explain how it can contribute to the retirement lifestyle you want to live.

Typically, married employees entitled to a pension will need to choose one of two options. A 100-percent option means the employee would take all their monthly pension amount when they retire. When they die, his or her spouse will receive nothing. Alternatively, they could choose a 50-percent option in which half the pension is left to their spouse after their death.

Consider working part-time.

By combining income from a smorgasbord of options—Social Security, retirement accounts like a 401(k) or an IRA, and pensions—you should be able to create the type of retirement you envision. Each of these income sources distributes funds in different ways. A financial advisor can help you determine a distribution strategy to provide the income you need while preserving the funds over the long term.

Maybe you'll want to keep working—full- or part-time. Some people love it and have no intention of stopping. I applaud them. I hope they can work for as long as they want. I have heard stories of people who reach the age of 100 and still show up at the office every day.

Others may need to work part-time because they need the money. Saving throughout your adult life will give you the choice to work or not work. And if you are working when you're older, I hope you find work you enjoy.

Whatever your reason—because you need to or want to—keep in mind that your ability to do so gets harder to count on as you age. Some people can keep going well into their 80s or even their 90s. But others encounter health problems and, no matter how firm their plans, simply can't.

Should I pay off my mortgage?

If you have a big mortgage on your home, should you take a chunk out of your retirement investments to pay it off before you retire? Maybe, but you might want to think about it. If you did that, you'd have less income because you'd have depleted your income-producing assets by a large amount.

I met with a couple in their mid-60's who were getting ready to retire. They still had a big mortgage payment with a high interest rate. Instead of taking money out of their retirement assets to pay it off, they chose to refinance their 30-year mortgage. Interest rates were very low, they didn't plan on moving, so it was less expensive for them to obtain a mortgage and continue making the payments that were already included in their budget. Pulling funds out of their investments would have resulted in less income and less flexibility. It is ideal to have your home paid off before you retire, but although this couple didn't have the assets to pay off their mortgage, they had enough income from pensions and social security to support a mortgage payment. This was the right solution for them.

The best scenario is to pay off debts before retirement. Depleting assets when you're no longer producing income can be risky. So buy your newer car, complete your major projects, and get your investments set up for a reliable cash flow.

What about retiring early?

Many people are in a position to retire earlier than expected. Sometimes, business owners sell their businesses before age 60. In other instances, employees are offered buyouts and are forced to decide whether to retire early or find another job. There's a lot to think about before making the leap.

When people retire before 59.5, they sometimes choose to leave some money in their 401(k) for emergencies. The rest they will put into a Rollover IRA. Whether retiring from a company or leaving for another job, money can be withdrawn from a 401(k) at age 55 without paying a 10% penalty. The ability to access this money earlier than age 59.5 makes it ideal to use as an "emergency" fund—a good strategy when retiring early.

You may be wondering why you should bother to roll over your money to an IRA if it can be accessed directly from your 401(k) at age 55. That's a good question, with a good answer. When you are retired, you'll want a steady income stream. A 401(k) does not usually provide this. Instead, you have to send in a request every time you want to withdraw money. And then, the money is taxed! It is much more prudent, and investment-wise, to gradually take your income every month. This is something you can do with an IRA.

Retiring early also means you'll have to figure out where your medical coverage will come from. This can be quite expensive, so make sure you make some arrangements for funding before you choose early retirement. It's been said that after retirement, the money that used to go toward a mortgage is now spent on medical bills.

Have enough in emergency funds, and plan carefully for extra expenses. This is crucial since your retirement years have been extended. You will likely have to live more years on your retirement assets than those who retire at a more conventional age. It's a big step!

And of course, be certain that you are mentally ready for full retirement. Maybe it makes more sense to find another job to fill in the gap.

It's a lot to think about. And whether you can't wait to retire or you're simply protecting yourself from the unknown, you want to be prepared. There isn't one right way to retire, but there is a wrong way—that's when you fail to plan or to save for it throughout your adult life.

Retirement Planning Checklist

☐ Do you have enough income?

☐ Will your spouse have enough income if you pass away?

☐ If you plan to retire between the ages of 55 and 59.5, will you need to access your 401(k)?

☐ Do you need to roll over your 401(k) to an IRA (e.g., cost, keeping control, investment choices, consolidation)?

☐ Do you have six months of income in an emergency account?

☐ Is your debt paid off?

☐ Do you have an intermediate fund (for travel, medical expenses, and extras)?

☐ Have you consulted with a tax expert for any tax issues that we may not have addressed? Investment professionals often seek advice from tax professionals and work as a team.

☐ Have you discussed Social Security options with a qualified professional?

☐ Have you discussed health insurance and Medicare options with a qualified professional?

☐ Have you discussed your pension options and the benefits of life insurance with a qualified professional?

☐ Have you discussed required minimum distributions with a qualified professional?

☐ Have you discussed Roth conversions with a qualified professional?

☐ Have you discussed beneficiary designations with a qualified professional?

"Think of estate planning as your family's guidebook for when you are no longer in the picture."

—*Jill Gleba*

CHAPTER 9

Taking Care of Yourself and Others

We've spent a lot of time talking about the income you'll need during the latter part of life. But let's be candid: When you're older, money won't be your only need. It may not even be the primary one. As you age, access to health care becomes critical—and expensive. It's not a comfortable conversation, but I won't do you any favors if I leave it out. Even more uncomfortable is talking about a plan for your own death. And we'll get to that, too.

I had an elderly client with three adult children. As she aged, the daughter who lived closest provided the extra care she needed. The daughter's health, however, was also declining. With both of them suffering medically, the daughter called upon her siblings for help. Unfortunately, the siblings couldn't step up, and she was forced make the hard decision to put her mother into an assisted-living home. She was well cared for there, and everything was going along fine until two siblings began visiting and asking for records and expenses. The mother and daughter were both clients of mine and, fortunately, we'd kept impeccable records. The siblings were appeased and grateful. Mom received great care until her death. After she passed, the siblings split the estate three ways, and there were no arguments. The mother had always talked openly about what assets she had and what should happen after she passed. The siblings didn't always agree with her wishes, but that didn't matter. It was all in writing, and her wishes were followed until her death. This is an ideal scenario. But we all know that when it comes to money, this isn't always the case.

Estate planning seems to have the connotation that it's for "rich" families, those with a lot to leave behind after their death. Instead, think of it as your family's guidebook for when you are no longer in the picture. Sound important? I think so!

Writing a will is not limited to what happens to your house, car, company, or other assets after you die. It also encompasses the question of who will take care of your children and who will be their guardians. Other instructions may include a list of your advisors, your burial instructions, and who will oversee the settling of your estate.

Estate planning is about:

- Securing your assets.
- Leaving instructions and wishes.
- Protecting your family or heirs.

These documents should be signed, notarized, and filed, making certain that the contents are fully and legally enforceable.

What happens if I don't plan my estate?

If you leave no specific instructions, default rules will apply upon your death and other living family members and government representatives will decide for you. Of course, that won't always be in your best interest. Here's a rundown of the consequences of not writing a will:

- Your burial preferences may not be honored. Whether you prefer cremation or a traditional burial, those you leave behind can decide based on convenience or their preferences.

- Your properties could be managed by someone you don't trust. If you don't have an appointed executor to your will, a clueless family member may be tasked with filing taxes, transfers, and managing your estate. Unfortunately, many don't know how to do these things properly.

- Some of your loved ones may not get an inheritance. Under the Interstate Succession Act, common-law marriages are not recognized. As a result, your partner may not get a portion of your estate.

- Your organization of choice may be cut from receiving donations. While many people spend their lives supporting charities, it is unfortunate that their tradition of giving ends with their death. If you're committed to leaving a legacy, your organization of choice should be listed in your will.

- The government will assign guardians for your minor children. If no parent is left and the children are orphaned, social services will step in and appoint a guardian. Unfortunately, there have been many stories of abuse or misuse of funds, even if the guardian is a relative. So, make sure you name someone you trust wholly.

- You can no longer put up a trust fund for your children. Upon death, assets are typically liquidated or sold to pay for debts, taxes, or processing fees. This means that if you have no specific instructions about saving a portion for your children, they will have nothing by the time they become of legal age.

What are the advantages of estate planning?

Aside from skipping all the consequences mentioned above, estate planning can also save your family a lot of trouble and a lot of money. A detailed document with your instructions will alleviate hassle and provide comfort while your loved ones recover emotionally from their loss.

The following are the top reasons why you need to plan these things:

- It can help skip the process of "probate," which would entail validating your will, paying off any remaining taxes and bills, and finally distributing remaining assets or amount to your family.

- You can avoid additional taxes. Once someone passes away, their properties are subject to a massive sum of taxes such as inheritance taxes and federal estate taxes. If you set up a trust between you and your spouse, you can lessen the transfer taxes or eliminate them entirely. Those who are elderly or have been diagnosed with terminal diseases may want to transfer their properties ahead of time to avoid such hassle.

- You can choose who will care for you and manage your finances if you become unable to make decisions for yourself due to illnesses, old age, or if you become mentally incapable.

- You can appoint a trusted guardian for your children. Should your young children be orphaned, you can name someone you trust to be their guardian. This doesn't necessarily need to be a family member as long as they qualify and prove their capacity to raise your children.

- You will avoid gold diggers. Some family members are in it for the money, so you must write these people off your will. Through proper and early estate planning, you can ensure that the people you love and care for receive what you want them to.

Estate planning is crucial to securing a comfortable life for your loved ones. More importantly, it will help them get through difficult times without having to worry about the assets you leave behind.

Even if you are younger, I hope reading this prompts you to talk with your parents and to get your own affairs in order, too. Many young couples think about a will or trust when they become new parents. A guardian (and some backups) must be chosen. They'll also need to decide how to distribute money to their young children and who will oversee the distribution in the event of their passing.

What if I need long-term care?

Another hard topic to consider is the possible need for long-term care during your golden years. Medicare serves as basic health insurance for the elderly, but it doesn't cover long-term care, and that can be extremely expensive. So, how do you plan for it?

With advance planning, there are options. If you don't prepare, your choices will be limited—and none will be appealing.

There is insurance that can cover expenses, but the time to buy a policy—just like any other insurance policy—is before you need it. You may be hesitant to spend money on protections you may never need. That's human nature. But human nature isn't always your friend. Dealing with the anguish of long-term health needs is bad enough. Not having the means to pay for them makes it that much worse. Get an insurance policy, and do it while you're still healthy. Seek the advice of a professional, and don't base your decision solely on something you read in a book—not even this one.

Like most insurance policies, options vary. Basically, though, you're agreeing to pay a monthly premium in exchange for the promise that, if you need it, the insurer will pay for your long-term care, either at home or in a facility. Understand exactly what's included in any policy you're considering.

For instance, a client in his 80s needed money to pay for help at home. He didn't need to be in a facility, and his long-term care policy had a "cash option" that provided money to pay for the help he needed in exchange for less in coverage in the future. This made sense for him.

Some policies offer a discount for couples. Some businesses offer long-term care policies as a group benefit employees can purchase. Business owners may be offered a credit or a write-off if they buy it or offer it to their employees.

Premiums can rise. Obtain the company's history of raising prices before you make your final decision to purchase.

Some policies allow you to insure against the cost of living. A policy may cover $5,000 per month, for instance, but offer the option to purchase a rider that increases the benefits with the cost of living.

If you don't like the idea of committing to a monthly premium, a hybrid policy is another option. This long-term care policy is combined with a life insurance policy or annuity. If you don't use the benefit, the premiums are paid to your heirs upon your death. It bothers me to lose premiums paid if they're never used, so I prefer this type of hybrid policy.

You could also choose to pay a lump sum for long-term care insurance instead of having a monthly bill. For instance, a sum of $100,000 may buy a benefit of $300,000 of long-term care insurance. Not everyone can afford this, but if you can, you'll get more bang for your buck. If you can spend $100,000 to receive $300,000 in benefits, it may be worth your effort.

The bottom line? Find out what's available, decide what's best for you, then buy what you can afford. Even if it isn't enough, it will help.

Maybe you're already covered.

Before you spend the money on a long-term care policy, check your existing life insurance policy. It may have a feature that will pay out a long-term care benefit if you end up in a nursing home instead of a death benefit. Also, a Health Savings Account (HSA) can be used to pay for your long-term care costs. An HSA is only available to those who have a high-deductible health care plan. If you do, it would be a good idea to fund this every year to help pay your future medical expenses.

Do I still need life insurance?

When you purchase life insurance, you're doing it because you love someone. You care about them enough to provide a tax-free lump sum that will take care of expenses. And there are many expenses to consider:

- Your final expenses (you want to leave this earth in style and with some dignity)
- Debt
- Mortgage
- College/Day Care expenses
- Emergency

These are things your loved ones will want to take care of immediately after your death. If you buy enough life insurance to pay for them, they will be grateful.

Consider whether your situation might dictate buying more insurance that will help replace your lost income. A $1,000,000 life insurance policy would provide income of $3,000 to $4,000 per month. This is a good strategy if you have children, especially if your spouse stays home to care for them. This income could relieve the pressures of transitioning back into the workforce.

When should you buy a policy? When you are young and healthy. Then keep it, even when you're older. If you and your spouse both collect Social Security checks, you will lose the lower of the two incomes when one of you passes away. The life insurance policy you kept can help replace the loss of the second income.

If you have a term policy at work, find out if you can convert this policy into something permanent. Usually, you can do this without proving insurability or having to pass medical tests. Many people who are not healthy will convert term insurance policies to a permanent policy to supplement their spouse's income.

Estate planning is a gift for your heirs.

Estate planning is a kind gesture for your heirs. Our firm helps clients using a three-page document that identifies:

- Income and where it comes from
- Insurance policies (life, health, disability, long-term care, home/auto, and business)
- Bank accounts
- Investment accounts
- Home and real estate
- Debt

Heirs benefit by finding the information they need all in one place. It also allows a financial planner to help them settle the details more easily. It's a difficult time; you can make it easier by taking the time to prepare.

Part of estate planning is understanding the potential impact of estate tax. As of this writing, estate tax only applies to estates valued above $11.7 million, so most individuals will not have to consider taxes. But keep in mind that all assets in your estate apply to the value, not just cash.

If your estate is worth more than $11.7 million (or if tax laws change and the threshold is reduced), you can strategize ahead of time to reduce future estate taxes. An elder-care attorney specializing in trusts and estates can team up with you and your financial planner to develop a strategy.

The $11.7 million threshold is a significant problem for many small-business owners. Many small businesses have assets worth more than that, but these assets are not liquid assets. When the owner dies, the assets must be liquidated to pay estate tax—in other words, the business must be sold. They could have redirected some of the assets into the cost of elder care when they were still living. A tax attorney can advise you with these types of moves.

Getting past the guilt of inherited wealth.

A young man came into our office. His parents had recently passed away, and he'd received a large inheritance. He was grieving the loss of his parents, and the loss of the support they'd always provided. Sure, he was financially secure now. But he was also feeling an overwhelming sense of guilt.

He confided to his best friend that he knew he should have been excited about the inheritance, but instead felt guilty. The friend was unsympathetic: "What a problem to have! You could give me the money; that should take care of your guilt."

His friend's reaction exacerbated his feelings. "The feeling of guilt is wrong, it's not normal," he told himself. Instead of dealing with his feelings in a healthy manner, he internalized them and tried to ignore their existence.

If you've inherited wealth, maybe you can relate. You might find yourself struggling with guilt since it came as a result of the death of a loved one. It's not often discussed. You're supposed to be happy with a windfall of money, right? Expressing guilt may seem insincere or be perceived as a lack of gratitude. But it's a real emotion, and it needs to be addressed. We often encourage our clients to visit a therapist.

Guilt is a powerful and negative emotion that makes one feel as if they did something wrong. It can corrode thinking for years, even a lifetime, unless it's clearly understood and treated.

We talk with our clients who receive inheritances and encourage them to look at their newfound wealth as a blessing, not a curse. If they recognize feelings of guilt, we ask them to explore the reasons they feel this way. Here are some possibilities:

- Someone had to pass away for them to get the money.
- It doesn't feel right because they didn't earn the money.
- They fear they might do something wrong with the money.
- They fear the grantor wouldn't approve of what they do with the money.
- They fear other living family members won't approve of what they do with the money.

As our discussion continues, we remind them that the inheritance is a gift, and we help them uncover opportunities they wouldn't otherwise have. We explore possibilities by asking questions like this:

- If you could do anything with the money, without fear or guilt, what would you do?
- What would be a healthy perspective for you to create or adopt regarding the wealth?
- What fears about the wealth do you need to overcome or let go?
- How has the wealth made you grow personally?
- How has the wealth blessed you in a surprisingly good way?
- What are you thankful for?

Seeking answers to these questions can help them move past negative feelings. It can help them find ways to align dreams and visions with their current reality and free them of the guilt associated with inheriting money. Only then are they ready to set goals and discuss ways to invest the money according to their values and wishes.

The complicated inheritance tax rules.

Tax codes and IRS rules are very complicated, and I won't dive into all of them here. There are certain rules for married people, and another set for single people. Other hurdles arise based on the type of asset involved. An IRA, real estate, bank accounts—they all have different guidelines. An attorney, tax professional, and a financial planner can work together on your behalf to figure it all out.

Have a plan and an up-to-date will!

When putting your own estate plan together, work with experts in the field (not your corporate attorney uncle). Search out an estate-planning attorney to help with wills and trusts, an elder-care attorney to help with Medicaid and health care planning, and a special-needs attorney if you have a family member with special needs. This group of experts will ensure that the plan you envision is executed.

Make sure you have an up-to-date will. This is important.

Prince died in 2016. As of the writing of this book, his estate remains unsettled because he died without a will. His sister and five half-siblings are still working out how they will divide his estate. To make matters worse, the siblings have signed portions of their estate rights over to various companies, and all these parties are fighting it out in court.

A will could have prevented all of this.

Get advice, check it twice.

When you interview a financial planner, CPA, accountant, or attorney, please be sure to get more than one opinion, even if it costs you. I have made this mistake myself. I hired an attorney for a business transaction. I took the attorney's idea to my CPA, who informed me that it wouldn't work. I then had to hire a second attorney, and pay for the transaction twice.

Here's another example of the value of a second opinion. A long-time client called our office. He wanted to withdraw more than $1 million dollars from his portfolio and move it to an irrevocable trust. This alarmed me, since an irrevocable trust is a kind of trust that cannot be changed or canceled after the document has been signed. I asked him to come in. When he did, we consulted a second attorney.

Here's what we determined in that consultation:

- Withdrawing the money for the trust would incur a significant tax expense.
- The trust restrictions would prevent him from selling his home and moving to his cottage.
- Many additional restrictions were uncovered as we discussed the pros and cons of creating this type of trust.

Fortunately, my client only lost the initial fee when he decided not to go through with the funding of the trust. The first attorney was selling him a product without taking the time to understand his goals, situation, and what type of assets would be sold to fund the trust. This story is not intended to provide legal advice but is here to illustrate how crucial a second opinion can be.

For you, special-needs caregivers.

If you care for a family member with special needs, you need to consider what will happen to them when you pass or are no longer able to provide the care they need.

Life insurance helps. Couples with a special-needs family member often choose a Second to Die policy. With this policy, the proceeds can go into a "special needs trust" filling in the financial gaps that can arise after the caregivers pass. The trust can be used for various expenses and won't affect the amount of a monthly disability check. There are limitations, so see a lawyer who specializes in this type of work before making your purchase.

An Achieving a Better Life Experience (ABLE) account is something else family members caring for someone with special needs could consider. Contributions can be deposited into the account each year. It is specifically for the care of the person with special needs. Contributions and the account balance have limits, so it's best to work with a financial advisor. They can help you keep the account compliant with the rules.

Qualified expenses aren't limited to medical expenses. It can also cover things like:

- Education
- Housing
- Transportation
- Employment support
- Personal support
- Health and wellness
- Financial management
- Legal assistance
- Overnight monitoring
- Funeral and burial

Caregivers have a lot to think about. It's important to preserve benefits that offer safety and security, a social life, and the ability to be around family. There are many who can help navigate the ins and outs—attorneys, financial planners, CPAs, and a trustee.

What happens if you are the sole caregiver for a person with special needs? It is important to know who will become the caregiver when you, as the primary caregiver, passes. It creates a big challenge for others. I have two special-needs brothers, and I oversee the care of the oldest. When my husband and I pass, I designated my younger son (I have 2 adult kids) to care for his uncle. "Won't Michelle do it, since she is the oldest?" he asked.

"Nope. Michelle is taking care of our estate and you live closer to him," I responded. "This is your responsibility." Now it's understood, and I'm glad we had that talk!

There are lots of things you can do to prepare for the time when you are no longer able to be the sole caregiver. If you can, choose your successor ahead of time. Document all of the details of the person's care—their personal information, habits, typical day, favorite foods, close friends and family members, hobbies and favorite activities, and medical and financial details. This will make your successor's life easier if something happens to you.

It'll also give you some comfort to know the person to whom you'll pass the baton when you die. Before they passed away, my parents cared for my brothers. They knew several of us were ready to step up when we were needed. It gave them a sense of relief and it made the transition easier.

Plan for the care of aging parents.

It's difficult to deal with the death of a loved one—especially a parent. It's also challenging to take on the care of elderly parents.

I often see the responsibility fall on one or two family members while the rest step back. There should be one person in charge of medical and financial matters, the other duties can be split up among family members—if you're lucky. Conflicts often arise when a "helper" in the family wants to take over after the main caretaker has been in that position for several years. Exhaustion and emotional stress add fuel to the fire. Planning could prevent some of this. Find out your parents' wishes and have a game plan in place before these things arise.

It makes sense to me to designate one person to sign documents, sell the home, settle the estate, and make sure things get done after parents pass on. Leaving the responsibilities to several siblings opens the door to different opinions, and conflicts are practically inevitable.

Frequently, I will see a home left to siblings. One sibling—who may not have the means to buy the others out—feels entitled to live in the home as a partial owner. The other siblings feel slighted, and the trouble begins.

Have a clear, targeted discussion before a parent passes. Find out what your parents want to happen after they're gone. It's their estate, after all. They can do with it what they want. Your job is to fulfill their wishes.

What you need, when you need it.

If you're a caregiver, know where to find your loved one's financial information, including bank accounts, investments, and insurance policies. Don't stop there. Find out where they keep their medical records. Make a list of their doctors and dentists. Know where to find their wallet and put together a list of friends, passwords, and any other everyday items that might be important.

I had a client who had to take his mother to the emergency room. He had no idea where to find her purse, insurance card, patient advocate paperwork, power of attorney, or will. Imagine the sinking feeling you'd have if a hospital needed a decision, and you had nothing to prove that you were the designated helper.

Don't be afraid to talk to your parents, aunts, uncles, children, or anyone in your care. My grandmother used to put stickers under her furniture that told us who was supposed to get each item when she passed. At the time, we found this to be somewhat morbid. But it made her feel good to know that her things were taken care of. She made it easier for my mom and her sister to distribute her belongings to the many family members and friends she'd loved after she passed. She even left her bowling ball to her best friend! Her planning made those of us she'd left things to feel special. She'd thought about what she wanted each of us to hold onto in her memory. By putting her wishes in writing, she'd ensured that there was no confusion or difficulty deciding what to do with her estate after she was gone.

Caring for yourself and for others gets trickier as we age, but planning helps. Plan for your own care and for the care of loved ones.

When should you start? You guessed it! *Now.*

AFTERWORD:
What's Next?

You can't always get what you want
But if you try sometimes, well, you just might find
You get what you need

—The Rolling Stones

I hope you're pumped up and excited to start practicing the skills of investing and aspire to a lifetime of learning.

I hope it leads to a successful retirement on your own terms.

I hope your attitude toward money is beginning to change for the better.

And I hope you're ready to share what you've learned with the next generation.

I want investing to be a normal, everyday activity that is discussed openly—even the mistakes. We'll all make some. It's okay, as long as we just keep trying.

Just keep trying.

Many people feel that no matter how hard they work, they just can't get ahead. They know there must be a better way, but they sure don't know what it is. They don't know because they were never taught. Or worse yet, they learned bad habits from their parents. To be fair, their parents likely didn't have the knowledge or expertise to train them. And this valuable information is almost never taught in school. So where could they have learned it?

If this sounds like you, don't worry. Start now, and just keep trying.

Ideally, we should save for retirement throughout our 30+ working years. The money we save might need to last for 30+ years of retirement. As lifespans get longer, having enough savings to last gets more difficult. But any effort is worthwhile. Even if you're starting late, don't panic! Start now, and just keep trying.

You can prepare now by giving up a few less-important things and putting some money aside to invest. It will make a difference in your life. I've seen it for myself—over and over—for 35+ years. When you choose your house, your car, and how often you cook at home instead of eating out, you are also choosing how much you can save and how well you can prepare for your future.

So start now!

Your habits, beliefs, and interests are a combination of the people you choose to be with, the advice you choose to heed, and the thoughts you choose to embrace. Something led you here, to this place, to this book with which I'm encouraging you to think about your spending, saving, and investing habits. You can work for your money, and by investing, you can also make your money work for you. If you didn't know it before, you know it now. And now is the time to begin.

Adjust your cash flow, spend your money on the things you value, and let things go that are not important. Before you know it, you'll realize that you have enough saved that you're able to retire and enjoy life.

It's two simple steps: spend less, save more.

Spending less and saving more are all it takes to start on the road to financial security. Even if you're not feeling 100% confident yet, take a small step.

Doing something is always better than doing nothing. If money is tight, if you're struggling to pay monthly bills, seek professional help. There is no shame in this. A professional can help you; it's what they do. As long as you can change the way you think about money, you can turn things around.

Remember, just keep trying!

No extra money? Maybe you can improve or change your career. If you feel you are not where you "should be," talk to your boss, a coworker in a higher position, a career counselor, or a recruiter. They may have advice for you. Just don't be complacent. Find a profession that you enjoy—and one that pays you what you deserve.

Don't get distracted, it all starts with that first step.

Get your team together.

Interview tax professionals, financial planners, and estate-planning attorneys. Find experts who make you feel comfortable and who work with people in your situation. If you're searching on behalf of a parent, an elder-care attorney may be suitable. A special-needs attorney makes sense if you're caring for a special-needs person. Creating assets and handling them is a responsibility that takes thought and care. You want the right people on your team.

Begin your journey to wise investing.

No matter how old you are, you can invest for the future.

Choose investments and risk based on how much time you have before retirement, your personal goals, and your comfort level. Remember, you are choosing your own "ride," but you can't control what the market does. Nobody can. And nobody can predict it with consistent accuracy either. Just keep up those monthly deposits. Stick with it. Get comfortable with being uncomfortable. You can't control everything in life, but you can just keep trying.

Find a coach! My own kids and my clients have the benefit of having me as their coach. Investing in the market consistently without reacting to outside sources is ingrained in their behavior. They save 10-20% of their income because that is what they were taught. They ignore media and hype. It takes training, and it takes time to get used to letting go of the emotions. Sure, sometimes it's frustrating. You won't always get the immediate results you're looking for. Keep this in mind, but invest anyway.

Just keep trying!

There is more to life—and retirement—than money. It includes a great social life with friends and family, good health, and planning your legacy. So do what brings you joy—stay curious, be active, find hobbies. If you want to go on four vacations every year and retire at age 65, then do it! If you want to retire earlier and only take one vacation per year, go for it! Invest wisely now so you can choose your own retirement adventure.

Take good care of yourself and your loved ones.

"Spending less and saving more are all it takes to start on the road to financial security."

—*Jill Gleba*

About the Author

JILL GLEBA grew up outside Detroit, Michigan, and founded Gleba and Associates, an independent financial management firm, more than 35 years ago. As an Accredited Investment Fiduciary (AIF), Jill has helped many businesses, employees, and families save and invest for their futures. Over the years, Jill found that many people weren't taught to invest money, and she feels strongly that investing should be "common sense"—as normal as driving a car. Her goal is to change this pattern for every working family.

As a certified woman business owner, Jill has consistently been presented the 5-star award, recognizing her as a top financial planner in Metro Detroit. She has been featured in both *Hour Detroit* and *Detroit Monthly* magazines, has been a guest on many radio and television segments, and has been an invited speaker at many events.

She is a board member of Furniture Bank and lives with her husband Bruce. They both enjoy the outdoors, traveling, golfing, and spending time with their adult kids (Michelle and husband Nick; Robert and partner Courtney) and their children's dogs.

To learn more about Jill and her work, visit her website: jillgleba.com.

About the Illustrator

COURTNEY WOLLET is an artist and illustrator based in Ann Arbor, Michigan where she lives with her partner, Robert, and their two dogs. She developed a love of visual storytelling while studying Art and Design as well as Communications at the University of Michigan. Through her illustrations, she tells the story of the little moments that give meaning to, and breathe a little adventure into, our everyday lives.

To see more of her work, visit her website: courtneywollet.com.